the unofficial Harry Potter COOKBOOK

 CookNation

THE UNOFFICIAL Harry Potter COOKBOOK

OPEN UP THE CHAMBER OF SECRET RECIPES: IDEAL FOR SORCERERS, PRISONERS, GOBLINS, WIZARDS, CURSED CHILDREN & MUGGLES

ISBN 978-1-912511-48-8

DISCLAIMER

~ CONTENTS ~

Great Hall Dinners 45

Decree Desserts

Sorcerer's Snacks & Drinks

Turn food into magic with these Harry Potter Inspired Recipes

Hello-hamora and welcome!

Who can forget the scrumptious feasts at Hogwarts? Tables groaning under plates and dishes of the most delicious food, and you can only imagine the tempting aromas wafting around the corridors of the castle. Sounds like hard work too doesn't it?

In fact, thanks to food being one of the five principal exceptions to Gamps Law of Magical Transformations, creating a fabulous meal is not something you can produce by magic. You could use your magic wand – if you have one - to help with the preparation, but the real creative work is down to you. The effort is worth it though. Smiling faces because of full tummies is always a joy to see. To make food prep easier and to produce some fabulous food, this collection of Harry Potter inspired recipes will have you shouting Merlin's pants and serving up dishes that will be (were)wolfed down in no time.

There really is nothing like feeling hungry. Not eating regularly makes you hangry and moody and complain like Ron Weasley with an empty stomach. There's no need to go on a forage for mushrooms you then stew to make an unappetising snack. There are so many great recipes in this book to make a magical meal.

 ## Meals for Every Day

Mrs. Weasley was such a whizz in the kitchen. Of course, she had her wand to help her chop, dice and stir. These recipes are easy enough that even muggles who are novice cooks can master them. The dishes will keep a hungry family – even one as large as the Weasley clan - full and happy.

Start the Day Right with a Healthy Hogwarts Breakfast

It is still said that breakfast is the most important meal of the day and it seems the wizarding world knows this too. They want the students to kick the day off well and the breakfast tables at Hogwarts are filled with bacon, cereals, porridge, eggs (scrambled and fried), sausages, fried tomatoes, kippers, rolls, toast, marmalade, milk, orange juice, pumpkin juice, tea, and coffee. Of course, you don't have an army of house elves in the kitchen to help out, so a muggle breakfast is less of a spread, but no less enticing with our delicious recipes.

Whether you're cooking breakfast for students who've been in the library all night looking for ways to breathe underwater for an hour or swatting for OWLS GCSEs, or a husband who's setting off by floo powder for another day at the Ministry of Magic Transport, a bowl of Peter Pettigrew's P-p-p-pecan Porridge or a plate of Newt Scamander's Scrambled Eggs will really set them up for the day. And for health-conscious mum, there's Avada Ked-Avocado Toast. So good, it will put all the other pics of Avo-toast on Instagram to shame.

Lock Up Hunger with a Legilimens Lunch

Lunchtimes will become a breeze. Easy to make, portable, but delicious food that stops tummies grumbling in the afternoon can be so boring when your imagination stops at sandwiches, especially if there's an appetite as large as Dudley Dursley's to be satisfied. Certainly, Ron didn't look forward to his squashy corned beef sandwiches on his first train to Hogwarts but there's no need to buy the entire contents of the sweet trolley as did Harry. Chocolate frogs, liquorice wands, and Bertie Bott's Every Flavour Beans do not make a healthy, filling lunch for growing boys, or indeed anyone. Anyone with a bottomless stomach like Ron's needs feeding! (Remember that scene in the Philosopher's Scone Stone movie when he had a chicken drumstick in both hands?).

Our lunch recipes are attention grabbing and scrumptiously good for the whole family. How about Gillyweed Sushi for a hipster teenager? Some Leek-y Cauldron Couscous for a vegetarian? Bathilda Bagshot's Baguettes will satisfy anyone. Everyone will look forward to opening their lunchbox to see what delight awaits.

Feast on Dinner Like a Wizard

You don't need lots of fancy ingredients or have to spend a fortune to feed a family with our recipes. You certainly won't have to resort to leaving money for eggs and milk at the farmhouse because you haven't eaten a decent meal for days. There's also no need to be fancy and fripperous every day. No one expects to come home to a flamboyant Great Hall style feast laid out on the dining table.

These recipes are built on ready-available ingredients at prices most households can budget for. The beauty lies in turning simple everyday ingredients into a great dish, as if by magic. They cover all tastes, so even the fussiest eater will to tempted to tuck in.

In the wizarding world, there's rarely a mention of tiredness (except poor Lupin when he has to cope with the rigours of his full moon changes). When you have a wand and can travel without moving a step it's easy to stay energetic. Not so for muggles. After a busy day, even just the thought of pulling together a family meal can be daunting. Open up this collection of recipes to find meals you can make in minutes and meals you can make at a more leisurely pace. From good old classics like Butterbeer Battered Cod & Chips to Mad Eye Moody's Mac & Cheese and Diagon Alley Ale Pie, there's plenty of choice for weekdays and weekends.

The recipes in this book will also take you on a culinary world tour faster than the Hogwarts Express (or faster than Snape can run away from shampoo!). We bring you Firebolt Fajitas to which you can add extra chillies if you want it as hot as dragon's breath, Cedric Diggory's Stir Fried Duck for a taste of the Orient (so good it would make Cho Chang cry – again!), and Spineless Lockhart's Spinach & Ricotta Cannelloni for a trip down Italy's memory lane.

Meals for Every Day of The Year

Whether the sun is shimmering on the waters of the Black Lake, or the steps to the owlery are slippery with ice, our recipes cover all seasons and every day of the year. Yule, you'll never be stuck for something to eat with our recipes. The only problem will be in deciding which to make first.

We have light but wholesome breakfasts for warm days and hearty, belly-warming breakfasts for days you want to keep out the cold and keep hunger locked up until lunchtime like a prisoner in Azkaban. We can offer a light but nutritious lunch perfect for summer to be eaten outside in the sunshine or hot, portable meals for when the weather is wintery. For dinner, take your pick from typical British fare or something more exotic, followed by desserts that look and sound far too good to eat. Add in our selection of snacks and drinks and every day is covered including brunch and supper.

Meals for Special Occasions

In the Harry Potter novels there are only a few major celebrations: Harry's seventeenth birthday, Bill and Phlegm Fleur's wedding, and Nearly Headless Nick's 500th Deathday Party are those we're furnished with most details about. The food at Nick's party could hardly be called celebratory and you can't even imagine serving up Maggoty Haggis, a slab of mouldy green cheese, or a grey cake in the shape of a tombstone. Mrs. Dursley's elaborate pudding (before Dobby dropped it on Mrs. Mason's head) or Harry's snitch-shaped birthday cake sound infinitely more tempting (let's not think too much about the squashed Happee Birthday Cake Hagrid gave Harry).

We can't promise that we'll make you so clever as to enable any of your guests to simply order what they want, and it magically appear as did the partygoers at the Yule Ball, but this recipe book contains a whole cauldron full of dishes just perfect for muggle celebrations. You can put together a fabulous menu for all kinds of parties and events including birthday parties, family barbecues, Easter lunch and Christmas dinner. There are recipes perfect for any Harry

Potter themed event, even a prom or wedding. Guests in fancy dress will love to tuck into a meal of Salazar Slytherin's Sesame Salmon, followed by Ron Weasley's Really Good Wellington with Godric Gryffindor's Gratin and a pudding of Chamber of Secrets Chocolate Sundae.

Of course, what could make Halloween even more spookily perfect than a table laden with lip-smacking dishes like Goblet of Fire Jambalaya, Dementor-ed Eggs and Patronus Popcorn, washed down with lashings of The Half Blood Prince's Potion and no chance of the feast being interrupted by Professor Quirrell and an ugly troll?

Whatever special occasion you are catering for, there are plenty of recipes to suit meat eaters, pescatarians, and vegetarians and whatever dishes you choose, they're sure to beat the Slug Club's dinner parties, even if the guests did get to tuck into huge bowls of profiteroles.

We promise you, there are no Weasley's Skiving Snackboxes or Hagrid's hard as rock, break your teeth, rock cakes here, so now it's now time to apparate onto the next roll of parchment to dive into our Harry Potter inspired recipes.

Enjoy!

TRADITIONAL
E~~NGLISH~~ HOGWART

Breakfasts

Ollivander's
Wand-erful Omelette

 ## Ingredients

- 1 tsp olive oil
- ½ onion, finely chopped
- ½ red pepper, finely chopped
- 50g/2oz mushrooms, sliced
- 1 tomato, finely chopped

- 3 eggs
- 1 tbsp milk
- Salt & black pepper
- 2 tbsp grated cheddar
- 1 tsp fresh parsley, chopped

Method

1 Heat the oil in a medium-sized skillet over medium-high heat. Add the onions, peppers, mushrooms and tomatoes, and fry for 2 minutes. Remove vegetables and set aside. This will be the 'core' of your omelette.

2 Crack the eggs into a bowl, and beat in the milk and a pinch of salt and pepper.

3 Add the egg mixture to the frying pan, again over medium-high heat. Move the eggs around the pan as they cook, pushing the cooked egg into the centre and allowing the runny egg to fill the space.

4 When the egg mixture is almost set, add the softened vegetables over one half the omelette, along with the grated cheddar, and fold in half.

5 Slide the omelette onto a plate, sprinkle with the fresh parsley, and serve to whichever wizard the omelette chooses.

Chef's Note

Although there's not a phoenix feather, unicorn hair or dragon heartstring in sight, Garrick Ollivander favours this veggie-packed omelette, as it sets him up for a day of crafting and selling the (according to Mr. Ollivander) best wands in the wizarding world.

Peter Pettigrew's P-p-p-pecan Porridge

SERVES 1

 Ingredients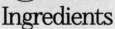

- 50g/2oz porridge oats
- 350ml/12½floz milk
  (full fat is Scabbers's
  favourite)
- ½ red apple, grated
- 1 tbsp pecans, chopped
- ½ tsp cinnamon
- 2 tsp maple syrup

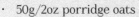 Method

1 Bring to boil in a small cauldron on the hob, and simmer for 4 minutes, stirring regularly. Alternatively put the oats and milk into a microwaveable bowl and heat on full power for 2 minutes

2 Meanwhile, add the pecans to a non-stick frying pan over a medium heat, and toast for 3 minutes.

3 Stir the grated apple and cinnamon into the porridge.

4 Add the toasted pecans, drizzle the maple syrup over the top, and serve. It's good enough for a rat!

Chef's Note

Back when Peter Pettigrew was known as 'Scabbers' - and lived a much more carefree and less despised life - Ron Weasley used to share this breakfast with his beloved pet rat. Ron now recoils in horror at the thought.

SLYTHERIN'S SALIVATING SMOOTHIE

Ingredients

- ½ cup rolled oats
- 250ml/1 cup coconut milk
- 1 frozen banana
- 1 cup blueberries
- 1 cup strawberries
- 1 cup spinach
- 1 tbsp honey

Method

1 Add all the ingredients to a food processor (or high-speed, self-stirring cauldron), and blend until smooth.

2 Taste the smoothie, and adjust the consistency and sweetness with more milk or honey if required (Salazar had a very sweet tooth).

3 Pour into 2 goblets, and serve.

Chef's Note

The best part about this smoothie for Hogwarts founder Salazar Slytherin was the tiny flecks of green, caused by the spinach, which, he said, glinted like emerald snake eyes. In some lights, it is believed he could even practise his Parseltongue whilst drinking it!

HAGRID'S GIANT FULL ENGLISH

Ingredients

- 4 sausages
- 4 rashers bacon
- 4 hash browns
- 12 cherry tomatoes
- 2 eggs
- 200g/7oz mushrooms, sliced

- 225g/8oz baked beans
- 4 slices bread (white or brown)
- 2 tbsp olive oil
- Salt & black pepper
- 300ml/10½floz fresh orange juice

Method

1 Preheat the grill to medium-high.

2 Put the sausages in a foil-lined tray, and grill for 15 minutes, or until cooked through. Add the tomatoes and mushrooms for the last 10 minutes. Be careful not to leave cooked sausages anywhere near Fang.

3 Meanwhile, heat a tablespoon of oil in a large frying pan and fry the bacon until crisp, and the hash browns until golden.

4 Remove the bacon and hash browns from the pan and add the bread, frying for 2 minutes on each side, until as golden as a Snitch.

5 Heat the baked beans in a saucepan on low-medium heat for 5 minutes.

6 Add the second tablespoon of oil to a large, clean frying pan on medium heat, and crack the eggs into it. Fry until the whites have set.

7 Divide everything onto 2 plates, season with salt and pepper, and serve with fresh orange juice.

Chef's Note

Hagrid's top tip is to turn the oven on low, and use it to keep each cooked part of the breakfast warm until everything's ready. He also let us into a little secret – he doesn't really divide this into 2 portions! But then, he is half giant, so we'll let him off...

MANDRAKE PANCAKES

SERVES 4

Ingredients

- 200g/7oz self-raising flour
- 1 tsp baking powder
- 1 pinch of salt
- 1 egg
- 300ml/10½floz milk

- 25g/1oz butter, melted
- 150g/5oz blueberries
- 1 tsp vegetable oil
- Maple syrup
- Ear muffs

Method

1 Combine the flour, baking powder and salt in a large bowl.

2 Beat the egg and milk together.

3 Make a well in the centre of the flour and pour in the egg, milk and melted butter. Whisk to make a batter. Stir in half of the blueberries – Professor Sprout usually has some good ones.

4 Heat the oil in a large frying pan. Pour in the batter in small dollops – approx. 1 tablespoon each. Cook for 2 minutes, and when the top of each pancake starts bubbling, flip and cook for another 2 minutes (this should make 10-12 pancakes).

5 Stack the pancakes and top with the rest of the blueberries, and maple syrup drizzled over. Be sure to put on your ear muffs before serving to a mandrake.

Chef's Note

Did you know? This delicious breakfast is one of the only things that can calm a screaming mandrake root. As the cry of a mandrake can be fatal to witches and wizards, being able to cook these pancakes well may one day save your life!

Common Welsh Green Dragon Rarebit

SERVES 1

 Ingredients

- 1 tsp mustard powder
- 3 tbsp beer
- 25g/1oz butter
- 2 tbsp Worcestershire sauce
- 175g/6oz mature cheddar
- Salt & black pepper
- 2 slices bread
- 2 egg yolks

Method

1 Mix the mustard powder, beer, butter and 1 tablespoon of Worcestershire sauce in a small pan over a low heat.

2 Stir in the cheese until melted, and season with salt and pepper. Remove from the hob.

3 Toast the bread under a medium-high heat on the grill.

4 Beat the egg yolks into the cheese mixture. Pour over the toasted bread, and grill until golden brown and bubbling.

5 Drizzle with the remaining Worcestershire sauce, and serve quickly - before the other dragons catch the scent!

Chef's Note

Charlie Weasley often makes this tasty breakfast for the dragons in his care (it is a particular favourite of the Welsh Green). The scaly ones enjoy it most when the toast is 'chargrilled', with a dollop of fiery chilli jam on the side.

Fleur Delacour's Delightful Croissants

SERVES 6

 Ingredients

- 500g/1lb 2oz strong white bread flour
- 7g/¼oz salt
- 75g/3oz caster sugar
- 7g/¼oz instant yeast
- 300ml/10½ floz water
- 300g/11oz butter
- 1 egg

Method

1 Be warned: This recipe's a bit trickier - but you don't get chosen to be a Triwizard Tournament champion by shying away from challenges!

2 Pour the flour into a mixer with a dough hook. Add the salt, sugar, yeast and water, and mix slowly for 2 minutes. Increase the speed and mix for a further 6 minutes, until the dough is stiff.

3 Tip the dough out and roll into a ball. Dust with flour, wrap it in clingfilm and chill in the fridge for 1 hour. Dust the surface with flour, then roll out the dough into a rectangle of approximately 60 x 20cm, and 1cm thick.

4 Roll the butter out to approximately 40 x 20cm. Place in the centre of the dough, and fold the edges of the dough over, so they meet in the centre of the butter.

5 Fold the dough in half, wrap in cling film and chill in the fridge for 30 mins.

6 Repeat rolling out the folded dough into a rectangle and folding it again (without adding more butter) two more times. Wrap in clingfilm and chill overnight.

7 The following day, roll out the dough into a rectangle, and trim the edges with a sharp knife. Cut the dough into 2 long strips, then cut each strip into 6 triangles.

8 Pull 2 corners of each triangle to stretch it. Starting at this stretched side, carefully roll each triangle into a croissant shape.

9 Tuck the ends of each croissant in, then arrange them on a tray lined with baking paper. Cover with cling film and leave to rise for 2 hours.

10 Pre-heat the oven to 200°C/400°F/Gas Mark 6. Beat the egg and use it to glaze the croissants, then bake the croissants for approximately 15 minutes, until golden brown. Cool on wire racks before serving.

Newt Scamander's Scrambled Eggs

SERVES 2

Ingredients

- 1 tbsp butter
- 1 small onion, diced
- ½ cup green pepper, diced
- ½ cup mushrooms, sliced
- 4 eggs

- ½ cup tomatoes, diced
- ½ cup parmesan, grated
- Salt & black pepper
- 4 slices granary bread

Method

1 Melt the butter over a medium heat in a large frying pan. Fry the onion, pepper and mushroom until soft. Transfer into a bowl/suitcase/Niffler bed for temporary storage.

2 Beat the eggs, and pour into the same pan, stirring gently until almost completely cooked.

3 Add the vegetables, and continue cooking until the eggs are firm.

4 Remove from the heat, stir in the tomatoes and parmesan, season with salt and pepper, and serve on the toasted granary bread.

Chef's Note

Famous for his unrivalled knowledge and appreciation of all magical creatures, Newt Scamander always favours meat-free meals. He enjoys these special scrambled eggs with a squirt of tomato ketchup from that old bottle at the bottom of his bottomless suitcase.

BUCKBEAK'S BREAKFAST BUNS

SERVES 16

Ingredients

- 2 cups flour
- ½ cup sugar
- 1 tbsp baking powder
- 1 tbsp butter

- 2 eggs
- ½ cup milk
- 1 cup raisins
- ½ tsp ground cinnamon

Method

1 Pre heat the oven to 170°C/325°F/Gas Mark 3

2 Combine the flour, sugar and baking powder in a large bowl.

3 Rub in the butter using your thumbs and index fingers.

4 Beat the eggs and milk together. Add this to the flour mix, and stir.

5 Add the raisins (these are like catnip to Hippogriffs).

6 Divide the mixture onto a greased baking sheet (1 tablespoon per bun). There should be enough for 16 buns. Sprinkle the cinnamon over the top.

7 Bake for 20-25 minutes, or until risen and golden. Serve warm, to a very appreciative Hippogriff!

Chef's Note

Hagrid used to make these delicious buns for his beloved Buckbeak every morning. They would enjoy them together by the pumpkin patch, and Buckbeak never minded if they were a bit burnt (always a good thing when Hagrid's cooking is involved).

Godric Gryffindor's Gallant Gallo Pinto

SERVES 2

Ingredients

- 3 cups rice
- 2 tbsp olive oil
- 1 onion, finely chopped
- 1 red bell pepper, finely chopped
- 2 cloves of garlic, finely chopped

- 2 cups tinned red kidney beans, drained (keep the water)
- Salt & black pepper
- 2 tbsp fresh coriander, chopped

Method

1 Cook the rice in a large cauldron for approximately 20 minutes.

2 Heat the oil in a skillet over a medium-high heat. Sauté the onion, pepper and garlic, until soft (just like Godric, really).

3 Stir in the drained red kidney beans, ½ a cup of the reserved bean water, and salt and pepper. Bring to the boil, then simmer until cooked through.

4 Stir in the cooked rice, and heat through. Add the chopped coriander, and serve.

Chef's Note

Before becoming one of the founders of Hogwarts, brave Godric Gryffindor travelled the world on gallant adventures. He discovered this recipe for Gallo Pinto during one particularly heroic quest to Costa Rica. To make this breakfast extra filling, serve with scrambled egg (we recommend Newt Scamander's!)

21

AVADA KED-AVOCADO TOAST

SERVES 1

Ingredients

- 2 slices sourdough bread
- 1 avocado
- 1 tsp olive oil

- 2 eggs
- Salt & black pepper

Method

1 Toast the bread (either a toaster, grill, or the Incendio spell work well for this).

2 Scoop the flesh of the avocado into a small bowl, and mash it with a fork.

3 Spoon half the smashed avocado onto each slice of toast.

4 Heat the oil in a frying pan and fry the eggs. And one to each slice.

5 Season with salt and pepper, and serve.

Chef's Note

Be very careful when pronouncing the name of this dish – there have been several reported incidences of witches and wizards causing flashes of green light and very nearly performing the killing curse on their breakfast buddies. Why risk it, you might say? Because it's too good not to!

CROOKSHANKS'S CRANBERRY GRANOLA

SERVES 10

Ingredients

- 400g/14oz rolled oats
- 200g/7oz mixed nuts
- 100g/3½oz sunflower seeds
- 150g/5oz dried cranberries
- 3 tbsp vegetable oil
- 400g/14oz honey
- 1 tsp cinnamon

Method

1 Pre-heat the oven to 150°C/300°F/Gas Mark 2.

2 Add the oats, mixed nuts, seeds and cranberries to a large bowl, and stir (it will look more like owl feed at this point – don't worry, it's supposed to).

3 In a separate bowl, mix together the oil, honey and cinnamon.

4 Combine with the dry mixture, and stir to ensure it is fully coated.

5 Spread the mixture out evenly on a thin baking tray.

6 Bake for 30-40 minutes, stirring regularly to ensure an even bake.

7 Allow to cool before serving to eager cats.

Chef's Note

Crookshanks loves this crunchy homemade granola with a saucer of his favourite, full-fat milk*. Hermione's dentist parents are particularly approving of this, because of the additional calcium this adds to his diet, encouraging strong and healthy teeth.
*Please note: This applies to magical cats only. Cranberry granola is not recommended for Muggle cats.

MOLLY WEASLEY'S FAMOUS WAFFLES

SERVES 6

 ## Ingredients

- 2 eggs
- 250g/9oz plain flour
- 450ml/15½ floz milk
- 7g/¼oz baking powder
- 20g/¾oz caster sugar
- 1 tsp salt
- 2 tbsp vegetable oil
- Cooking spray

Method

1 Pre-heat waffle maker. (Note: being a witch, Molly Weasley can make these with just her wand. You, however, dear Muggle, will need a waffle maker).

2 Beat the eggs in a large bowl. Add the flour, milk, baking powder, sugar, salt and vegetable oil, and beat until smooth.

3 Spray the waffle maker with cooking spray. Pour the mixture onto the waffle iron and cook until golden brown. Serve immediately (as if you'll have a choice!).

Chef's Note

One of the many reasons Harry loves The Burrow so much is Ron's mum's famous breakfast waffles. He finds there's nothing better than waking up in a wonky, chaotic, magical house, full of all your favourite people, to the smell of fresh waffles! Harry likes his with maple syrup.

LEGILIMENS

Nymphadora Tonks's Thai Noodle Soup

SERVES 2

Ingredients

- 125g/4oz rice noodles
- 750ml/3 cups chicken stock
- 75g/3oz chicken, sliced
- 1 lemongrass stalk, finely chopped
- ½ cup mushroom, finely sliced
- 2 garlic cloves, finely chopped
- ½ red chilli pepper, sliced
- 1 tbsp fish sauce
- ½ cup spinach
- 1 tbsp fresh coriander, chopped

Method

1 Add the rice noodles to a pan of boiling water, remove from heat and soak for approximately 10 minutes. Drain, rinse with cold water, and divide into 2 bowls.

2 Bring the chicken stock to the boil. Add the chicken, lemongrass, mushroom, garlic and chilli, and cook over a medium heat until the chicken is cooked through.

3 Remove from heat. Add the fish sauce, spinach and coriander, and stir.

4 Spoon over the rice noodles, and serve immediately. If you're a Metamorphmagus like Tonks, your hair may just turn pink with happiness!

Chef's Note

Nymphadora Tonks discovered this delicious soup recipe whilst on assignment in Thailand as part of her Auror training. She (all too briefly) used to make it for her beloved husband, Remus, to give him much-needed energy on the night of the full moon. Little known fact: Werewolves love noodle soup.

Hermione's Ham Sandwich

SERVES 1

 ## Ingredients

- · 1 tsp butter
- · ½ tsp wholegrain mustard
- · ½ spring onion, finely chopped
- · 2 slices thick, crusty bread
- · 1 leaf crunchy lettuce
- · 2 slices cooked ham
- · 1 tomato, sliced
- · 2 slices cheddar cheese
- · 1 tsp mayonnaise

Method

1 In a small bowl, cream together the butter, mustard and spring onion.

2 Spread this onto one slice of the bread.

3 Layer the lettuce, ham, tomato and pickle on top. Defend from Ron.

4 Spread the mayonnaise over the other slice of bread, and use to complete the sandwich. Enjoy!

Chef's Note

Anyone who knows Hermione Granger knows she's always far too busy reading books, being brilliant and saving Harry and Ron's lives to spend too much time cooking. This simple ham sandwich recipe is tasty, quick to make, and easy to take on the road when you're on the run from Voldemort!

BATHILDA BAGSHOT'S BAGUETTES

SERVES 2

Ingredients

- 1 tsp olive oil
- 125g/4oz fresh mushrooms, sliced
- 1 onions, chopped
- 1 cloves garlic, finely chopped
- ¼ tsp dried oregano
- Salt & black pepper

- ½ French baguette, cut lengthways
- ½ cup grated mozzarella
- ½ cup fresh basil leaves, chopped
- 2 large tomatoes, sliced

Method

1 Pre-heat the oven to 200°C/400°F/Gas Mark 6.

2 Heat the oil in a small cauldron and sauté the onions, mushrooms and garlic. Add the oregano and a pinch of salt and pepper, and stir.

3 Place the baguette halves on a baking tray, and sprinkle with half the mozzarella and basil leaves.

4 Add the cooked vegetables, the sliced tomatoes, and the remaining cheese.

5 Bake in the oven for 10 minutes, until the cheese has melted. Why not flip through A History of Magic whilst you wait?

6 Remove from the oven, garnish with the remaining basil leaves, and serve.

Chef's Note

After living alone for many years, Professor Bathilda Bagshot came to perfect the art of a quick lunchtime baguette-for-one. There was a time when she would make 2, and take them round to her neighbour in Godric's Hollow, Lily Potter, for a good old gossip whilst her baby son, Harry, slept.

Romilda Vane's Roasted Veggies

SERVES 4

Ingredients

- ¼ cup olive oil
- 1 tbsp fresh thyme
- 1 tbsp fresh rosemary
- 3 cloves garlic, finely chopped
- 2 tbsp balsamic vinegar
- Salt & black pepper
- 1 sweet potato, cubed

- 1 large potato, cubed
- 1 red onion, roughly chopped
- 1 courgette, sliced
- 1 butternut squash, cubed
- 225g/8oz baby carrots, halved
- 2 red bell peppers, de-seeded and sliced
- 12 cherry tomatoes

Method

1 Pre-heat the oven to 230°C/450°F/Gas Mark 8.

2 Add the oil, thyme, rosemary, garlic and balsamic vinegar to a large bowl, and mix. Season with salt and pepper.

3 Add all the chopped vegetables, and stir to coat thoroughly in the seasoned oil.

4 Pour the vegetables into a large roasting tin. Roast in the oven for 40 minutes or until the potatoes are soft. Daydream about Harry Potter while you wait.

5 Remove from the oven, and serve.

Chef's Note

During their sixth year at Hogwarts, whilst obsessed with Harry Potter, fellow Gryffindor Romilda Vane tried to slip Harry some love potion disguised in this dish (love potion, in certain lights, can be mistaken for balsamic vinegar). Luckily, Harry doesn't like butternut squash, and politely refused.

Cobb-led Street of Hogsmeade Salad

SERVES 4

Ingredients

- 2 eggs
- 4 slices bacon
- ½ head iceberg lettuce, shredded
- ½ head romaine lettuce, shredded
- 2 cups chicken, cooked and chopped
- 2 tomatoes, chopped
- 1 avocado, peeled and sliced

- ½ cup blue cheese, crumbled
- 2 chives, chopped
- 2 tbsp red wine vinegar
- 1 tbsp lemon juice
- 1 tsp Dijon mustard
- 1 tsp Worcestershire sauce
- Salt & black pepper
- 3 tbsp olive oil

Method

1 Add the eggs to a cauldron of boiling water for 10 minutes, until hard boiled. Remove and cover with cold water for 5 minutes. Once cooled, peel and cut them into slices.

2 Cook the bacon in a frying pan on medium-high heat, until crispy. Drain the fat, cool and crumble.

3 Toss the lettuces together and divide over 4 bowls (or less, if you have a duel with Voldemort coming up, and need extra sustenance!)

4 Arrange the chicken, tomatoes, avocado, bacon and blue cheese in rows on top of the lettuce. Sprinkle with the chives.

5 Make the dressing by whisking together the vinegar, lemon juice, mustard, Worcestershire sauce and a pinch of salt and pepper. Add the oil, and mix.

6 Pour the dressing over the salad, and serve.

Chef's Note

Hogmeade's take on the traditional Muggle recipe for Cobb Salad, this tasty lunch could briefly be found on the menu of The Three Broomsticks, during a short-lived period where they branched out into food to try to boost business during the Second Wizarding War.

PARVATI PATIL'S PITTA PIZZAS

SERVES 2

Ingredients

- 4 pitta breads
- 4 tsp sun-dried tomato purée
- 4 tomatoes, chopped
- 1 red bell pepper, deseeded and sliced
- 100g/3½oz closed cup mushrooms, washed and sliced
- 1 shallot, chopped
- 50g/2oz mature cheddar, grated

Method

1 Pre-heat the oven to 200°C/400°F/Gas Mark 6.

2 Spread the tomato purée over the pitta breads.

3 Arrange the sliced tomatoes, pepper, mushrooms and shallot over the pittas (you could also use pineapple, chilli, cooked meats, or any other common Muggle pizza topping).

4 Top with the cheese, and bake for 10 minutes, until the cheese is melted and bubbling. Serve and enjoy!

Chef's Note

Parvati Patil's Pitta Pizzas (try saying that 5 times after a few butterbeers!) were famous in the Gryffindor girls' common room. If you fancied a midnight snack – and, maybe, a confidential chat about Divination, the latest dress robes or boys – you could always count on Parvati.

NEVILLE LONGBOTTOM'S FULLY LOADED NACHOS

SERVES 6

Ingredients

- 1 tbsp olive oil
- 1 onion, diced
- 450g/1lb ground beef
- ½ tsp chilli powder
- ½ tsp paprika
- ½ teaspoon cumin
- Salt & black pepper
- 450/1lb tortilla chips

- 400g/14oz pinto beans
- 6 tomatoes, diced
- 1 jalapeño pepper, finely diced
- ½ bunch cilantro, chopped
- Juice of 1 lime
- 1 avocado, diced
- 1 cup sour cream
- 1 cup cheddar cheese

 ## Method

1 Pre-heat the grill.

2 Heat the oil in a large cauldron over a medium heat, and cook the onion until soft. Add the ground beef, and cook for 10 minutes. Stir in the chilli powder, paprika, cumin, and a pinch of salt and pepper. Set aside.

3 Make the salsa by mixing the other half of the onion, tomatoes, jalapeño, cilantro, lime juice and a pinch of salt in a bowl.

4 Spread half the tortilla chips over a large baking tray, lined with foil. Top with half the ground beef mixture, half the pinto beans, and half the cheese. Repeat for a second layer.

5 Cook the nachos under the grill until the cheese is melted and bubbling (approximately 3-5 minutes).

6 Remove from the grill, and top with large dollops of the salsa, avocado and sour cream. Serve immediately.

Chef's Note

Neville Longbottom was quite a catch really – brave, loyal, and an excellent cook! He would sometimes knock up these fully loaded nachos up before a Quidditch match, to share with Ron and Hermione whilst they cheered on Harry. A true gent.

GREAT HALL-OUMI WRAPS

Ingredients

- 1 onion, chopped
- 1 red bell pepper, deseeded and sliced
- 1 cup mushrooms, sliced
- 1 courgette, sliced
- 1 tbsp olive oil
- 1 tbsp paprika

- Salt & black pepper
- 250g/9oz halloumi, sliced into 12
- 150g/5oz Greek yoghurt
- 2 tbsp harissa paste
- 4 tortilla wraps
- Handful mixed salad leaves

Method

1 Pre-heat the oven to 220°C/425°F/Gas Mark 7.

2 Arrange the onion, pepper, mushrooms and courgette in a large baking tray. Drizzle with the oil, paprika and salt and pepper, and toss to coat.

3 Roast the vegetables in the oven for 30 minutes. Remember to put on your dragon hide gloves before removing them, as the dish will be very hot.

4 Heat a small amount of oil in a griddle pan over a medium heat. Add the slices of halloumi and cook for 3-4 minutes on each side, until lightly browned.

5 In a small bowl, mix the Greek yoghurt and harissa paste.

6 Warm the wraps for 10 seconds in the microwave. Down the centre of each wrap, layer a few salad leaves, some of the roasted vegetables, 3 slices of halloumi and a dollop of the harissa yoghurt. Fold the wraps closed, and enjoy!

Chef's Note

These delicious wraps were often served to Hogwarts students in the Great Hall for lunch during the summer months. Hermione was a huge fan – Ron, on the other hand, wasn't so sure, as the slightly 'squeaky' sound of halloumi always reminded him a bit too much of Scabbers.

Gillyweed Sushi

SERVES 4

Ingredients

- 400g/14oz sushi rice
- 4 tbsp caster sugar
- 2 tbsp rice vinegar
- 4 sheets Gillyweed (nori, to Muggles)
- ½ cucumber, finely diced
- ½ red bell pepper, finely diced
- 1 carrot, finely diced
- 1 small avocado, finely diced

Method

1 Soak the rice for 30 minutes in a cauldron with 750ml/1¼ pints of water. Then, bring to the boil and simmer for 10 minutes, or until all the water has been absorbed.

2 In a bowl, stir the sugar into the vinegar, until it dissolves. Pour this into the rice, and stir gently to coat.

3 Allow to cool for 20 minutes. The Glacius freezing charm can help speed this up.

4 To assemble the sushi, place a sheet of Gillyweed (nori) on a sushi mat. Spread ¼ of the rice over it, leaving a 1cm gap at the top. Add some of each of the diced vegetables in a line across the centre.

5 Roll the nori from the near edge, using the sushi mat, and seal at the far edge.

6 Divide each sushi roll into 6 pieces, and serve.

Chef's Note

PLEASE NOTE: The rice vinegar in this recipe causes Gillyweed to lose its magical properties. Many witches and wizards have fallen foul of this and nearly drowned after eating Gillyweed Sushi and mistakenly assuming their gills would appear when they threw themselves into deep water.

St John's-wort Soup

SERVES 4

Ingredients

- 3 tbsp olive oil
- 1 onion, finely chopped
- 2 cloves garlic, finely chopped
- 1 tsp ground cumin
- 225g/8oz yellow lentils

- 1lt/4 cups vegetable stock
- 1 bay leaf
- Juice of 2 lemons
- Salt & black pepper
- Handful fresh parsley, chopped

Method

1 Heat the oil in a large cauldron over a medium heat. Add the onion and fry until soft. Stir in the garlic and cumin, and cook for a few more minutes.

2 Add the lentils, vegetable stock and bay leaf. Bring to the boil, then simmer for approximately 30 minutes, until the lentils are soft. (Stir regularly to prevent sticking – no one, magic or Muggle, likes burnt lentils).

3 Remove the bay leaf, add the lemon juice and parsley, and stir. Season with salt and pepper, and serve.

Chef's Note

This soup is so-called because of its bright yellow colour. It is often served in the wizarding world with a sprig of St Johns-wort to garnish. A particularly warming soup, it is best enjoyed with crusty bread, cosied up in front of the fire in the Gryffindor common room during the winter months.

Norwegian Ridgeback Rice

SERVES 4

 Ingredients

- 1 tbsp olive oil
- ½ onion, chopped
- ½ red bell pepper, chopped
- 1 chicken stock cube
- ½ tsp cumin

- ½ tsp paprika
- ½ tsp turmeric
- ½ tsp chilli powder
- 2 cups rice
- 4 cups chicken stock

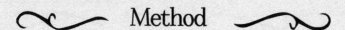 Method

1 Heat the oil in a large cauldron over medium-hot dragon fire. Add the onion, pepper, chicken stock cube, cumin, paprika, turmeric and chilli powder and fry until the onion is soft.

2 Add the rice and stir to coat.

3 Pour in the pre-mixed chicken stock. Bring to the boil, then simmer until the rice is cooked and the stock has evaporated (approximately 20 minutes). Stir regularly throughout to prevent sticking, adding more water if required.

4 Serve flamin' hot!

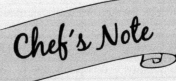 Chef's Note

This spicy rice recipe is so-called because of its fiery flavour. If you have Norwegian Ridgebacks in your care, you should make the rice even hotter by adding more chilli powder – dragons love spicy food, and Ridgebacks usually can't taste anything below 'medium-hot'.

Leek-y Cauldron Couscous

SERVES 2

Ingredients

- 125g/4oz couscous
- 1 tbsp olive oil
- 1 tbsp lemon juice
- 1 leek, sliced
- ¼ cucumber, diced
- 25g/1oz black pitted olives
- ½ red bell pepper, deseeded and sliced
- 6 cherry tomatoes, halved
- 150g/5oz feta, cubed
- Seeds from 1 pomegranate
- Handful fresh parsley, chopped

Method

1 Put the couscous in a large bowl and mix in the oil and lemon juice.

2 Add 150ml/5fl oz of boiling water, and leave to stand for 5 minutes. Fluff with a fork to separate the grains.

3 Meanwhile, cook the leek in a (non-leaky) cauldron of boiling water, until soft.

4 Drain, and stir into the couscous with the cucumber, olives, pepper, tomatoes, feta and pomegranate seeds.

5 Sprinkle with the fresh parsley, and serve.

Chef's Note

Couscous is a popular Muggle food, due to how easy it is to prepare (Muggles tend to be lazy when it comes to cooking – but then, they don't have magic to help, so who can blame them?) For this reason, couscous is also a favourite amongst Squibs, and wizards who didn't study hard enough in Charms class.

Tomato and Basil-isk Bruschetta

SERVES 3

Ingredients

- 6 large tomatoes, deseeded and finely chopped
- 5 tbsp olive oil
- 1 tsp balsamic vinegar
- ½ cup fresh basil leaves, chopped
- Salt & black pepper
- 1 loaf sourdough or ciabatta bread, sliced
- 2 cloves garlic, halved

Method

1 Pre-heat the grill to medium-high.

2 In a bowl, mix together the chopped tomatoes, 1 tablespoon olive oil, balsamic vinegar and basil. Season to taste with salt and pepper.

3 Place the slices of bread on a baking tray, and toast under the grill for 2 minutes on each side. If in a hurry, use the Incendio charm to speed things up.

4 Rub the cut garlic onto 1 side of each slice, then brush with the remaining olive oil to make garlic bread.

5 Spoon the tomato mix onto each slice, and serve immediately.

Chef's Note

This fresh and tangy bruschetta lunch is quick, mesmerising, and has a real bite to it – no wonder it's named after the basilisk! Poor Ginny Weasley still can't see this in a recipe book without shivering, and hastily flicking to the next page.

SCABBERS'S CHEESE & PICKLE SANDWICH

SERVES 1

Ingredients

- 2 slices bread
- 2 tbsp pickle
- 1 tbsp mayonnaise
- ¼ cup strong cheddar cheese
- ¼ red onion, sliced
- 20g/¾oz sundried tomatoes, chopped
- Small handful mixed salad leaves

Method

1 Spread the pickle over one slice of bread, and the mayonnaise over the other.

2 Layer the cheese, onion, tomatoes and mixed salad on one slice. Grate more cheese to replace what you've already eaten in your impatience.

3 Close the sandwich with the other slice, and enjoy!

Chef's Note

All rats love cheese, and Scabbers/Peter Pettigrew was no exception. But Scabbers wasn't content to make do with the occasional crumb dropped to him by Ron. He used to sneak down to the kitchen to make this posh cheese and pickle sarnie at night, whilst the Weasleys slept. Creepy.

SALAZAR SLYTHERIN'S SESAME SALMON

SERVES 4

Ingredients

- 4 skinless salmon fillets
- 2 tbsp honey
- 2 tbsp sweet chilli sauce
- 2 tbsp dry sherry
- 4 tbsp soy sauce

- 4 tsp ginger, finely grated
- 2 tsp sesame oil
- 1 tbsp sesame seeds
- 1 cup brown rice

Method

1 Pre-heat the oven to 200°C/400°F/Gas Mark 6.

2 In a shallow baking dish, mix together the honey, chilli sauce, sherry, soy sauce, ginger and sesame oil.

3 Lay the salmon fillets in the dish, and coat with the sauce. Leave to marinate for 15 minutes.

4 Sprinkle the sesame seeds on the salmon, and roast in the oven for 15 minutes, until cooked.

5 Meanwhile, cook the rice in a cauldron of boiling water.

6 Plate each fillet with half the rice, and serve. Obviously, make sure no Muggle-borns are present at the table.

Chef's Note

Before he left the school after a disagreement about the admittance of Muggle-borns, Salazar Slytherin used to make this healthy lunch for the four Hogwarts founders. Rowena Ravenclaw was a particular fan, as she believed salmon to be a brain-enhancing food.

Pre-Quidditch Quinoa Salad

SERVES 6

Ingredients

- 175g/6oz quinoa
- 3 tbsp olive oil
- 3 tbsp lemon juice
- 1 tsp Dijon mustard
- 2 cloves garlic, finely chopped
- 125g/4oz feta cheese
- 100g/3½oz cherry tomatoes, chopped
- 60g/2½oz black olives, halved
- ½ shallot, finely chopped
- 4 tbsp fresh parsley, chopped
- Salt & black pepper

Method

1 Add the quinoa and 480ml of water to a medium-sized cauldron. Bring to the boil and then simmer for 15 minutes, until all the water is absorbed. Remove from the heat, and let cool.

2 Meanwhile, mix together the olive oil, lemon juice, mustard and garlic in a small bowl.

3 Once it has cooled, transfer the quinoa to a large serving dish. Mix in the tomatoes, olives, feta, shallot and parsley. Season with salt and pepper.

4 Pour over the dressing, and serve. Quickly now, the match is about to start!

Chef's Note

This dish is so-called because quinoa is a source of protein, which translates into energy, and therefore the perfect pre-Quidditch lunch. Did you know, Quidditch matches can go on for days? According to Oliver Wood, the longest ever lasted 3 months - no wonder players need their quinoa!

PROFESSOR SPROUT'S SWEET POTATO & BEANS

SERVES 2

Ingredients

- 2 medium sweet potatoes
- 1 tsp olive oil
- 1 large onion, chopped
- 2 garlic cloves, finely chopped
- 1 tbsp brown sugar
- 1 tbsp red wine vinegar

- 2 tsp paprika
- 800g/1¾lb mixed beans in water, drained
- 400g/14oz chopped tomatoes
- 2 tbsp sour cream

Method

1 Pre-heat the oven to 200°C/400°F/Gas Mark 6.

2 Scrub the sweet potatoes and pierce the skins several times using a fork. Place on a baking tray, and bake for 45 minutes, or until cooked.

3 When the potatoes have been in for 30 minutes, heat the oil in a cauldron over medium-high heat, and fry the onion until soft. Add the garlic, sugar, vinegar and paprika and cook for a further 2 minutes.

4 Add the beans and tomatoes (get some fresh ones from the Herbology greenhouses!) and simmer for 5 minutes.

5 Slice each cooked potato in half. Spoon the bean mixture over, and serve with a dollop of sour cream on top.

Chef's Note

As any Herbology student who's paid an ounce of attention in class will know, Professor Sprout lives and breathes plants - and it's no different when it comes to her food. She tends to prefer Muggle vegetables, and the sweet potato is a particular favourite because it is low in calories, yet filling (and delicious!).

STUFFED KATIE BELL PEPPERS

Ingredients

- 4 red bell peppers, halved and deseeded
- 1 tbsp olive oil
- 1 small onion, finely diced
- 125g/4oz tomato couscous
- 1 small courgette, finely diced
- 75g/3oz tomatoes, chopped
- 3 tbsp fresh basil, chopped
- 125g/4oz mozzarella

Method

1 Pre-heat the oven to 200°C/400°F/Gas Mark 6.

2 Brush the peppers with a little olive oil. Place on a baking tray, and roast in the oven for 5 minutes on each side.

3 Meanwhile, heat the remaining oil in a cauldron over a medium-high heat, and cook the onion and courgette until soft.

4 Add the couscous, and cook for 1 minute. Pour in 200ml (7 fl oz) of boiling water, stir, and then remove from heat and let stand for 5 minutes.

5 Fluff the couscous with a fork and stir in the tomatoes and basil.

6 Spoon the couscous into the cooked pepper halves. Place a slice of mozzarella on top.

7 Place the peppers under the grill for 3 minutes, until the mozzarella is melted.

8 Serve hot or cold – both are equally good (just ask Katie!).

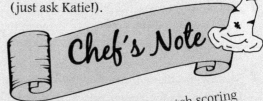

Chef's Note

After a hard Quidditch match scoring goals for Gryffindor and dodging Bludgers, Katie's go-to lunch was always her favourite; stuffed bell peppers. She was known to like them so much, it led to the other students nicknaming them, 'Katie Bell Peppers'. Kids can be cruel.

SIRIUS BLACK BEAN SOUP

SERVES 6

 Ingredients

- 1 tbsp olive oil
- 1 onion, chopped
- 2 carrots, chopped
- 4 cloves garlic, chopped
- 2 tbsp chilli powder
- 1 tbsp ground cumin

- 4 cups vegetable stock
- 800g/28oz (Sirius) Black beans
- 425g/15oz tinned sweetcorn
- 425g/15oz tinned tomatoes
- Salt & (Sirius) Black pepper

Method

1 Heat the oil in a large cauldron over a medium-high heat. Cook the onion, carrots and garlic until soft.

2 Stir in the chilli powder and cumin, and cook for 1 minute.

3 Add the vegetable stock, half the (Sirius) Black beans and the sweetcorn. Bring to the boil.

4 Meanwhile, blend the remaining beans and tomatoes in a food processor. Add this to the boiling broth, reduce the heat and simmer for 15 minutes. Plot revenge on Peter Pettigrew while you wait.

5 Shake off your anger, season with salt and pepper, and serve!

Chef's Note

Sirius never got to make his speciality soup for his godson, Harry, but if he had, we're sure it would have gone down well. It's best enjoyed with avocado and crusty bread, far away from Azkaban (Dementors quite like slurping on soup – it reminds them of the experience of sucking out a soul. Eeew.)

GREAT HALL

Dinners

Butterbeer Battered Cod & Chips

SERVES 4

Ingredients

- Sunflower oil for frying
- 900g/2lb potatoes
- 1 tsp salt
- 1 tsp black pepper
- 1 tsp garlic powder
- 225g/8oz plain flour

- 3 tsp baking powder
- 225g/8oz cod fillets, skinned and boned
- 285ml/10fl oz butterbeer (or just regular beer, for muggles)

Method

1 Pre-heat the oven to 110°C/225°F/Gas Mark ¼.

2 Pour sunflower oil into a large cauldron or deep fat fryer, and heat to 190°C /375°F.

3 Peel and slice the potatoes into chips. Cook in the deep fat fryer for 10 minutes, until golden brown. Transfer to a baking dish, and keep warm in the pre-heated oven whilst you cook the fish. Return the oil in the deep fat fryer to 190°C /375°F.

4 Mix the salt, pepper and garlic powder together. Rub this over the fish fillets to season.

5 Sift the flour and baking powder into the butterbeer, and whisk into a shiny batter. Dust the fish with flour, then lay it in the batter to coat.

6 Carefully place the fish in the deep fat fryer. Cook each fillet for 4-5 minutes, until golden. Once cooked, lay on kitchen paper to drain, then place in the oven to keep warm while you cook the other fish.

7 Serve fish with chips, and plenty of salt and vinegar. Enjoy!

Chef's Note

Butter beer makes an excellent base for the batter in this wizarding take on a muggle classic. It makes the fish so golden and inviting, you'd swear it must be magic! Harry likes his fish and chips with lashings of tomato ketchup, and mushy peas.

Harry Potter's One Pot Pasta

SERVES 4

Ingredients

- 350g/12oz spaghetti
- 350g/12oz cherry tomatoes, chopped
- 1 onion, chopped
- 1 red pepper, de-seeded & chopped
- 2 cups broccoli florets
- 4 cloves garlic, finely sliced
- 2 tablespoons extra virgin olive oil
- 1 litre/1½ pints water
- Salt & black pepper
- Grated parmesan

Method

1 Heat a large cauldron over a medium-high heat.

2 Add the pasta, tomatoes, onion, pepper, broccoli, garlic, oil and water, with a pinch of salt and pepper.

3 Bring the pot to the boil, and stir continuously for 9-10 minutes, until the water has almost evaporated.

4 Season with more salt and pepper, and serve with Potter's favourite - parmesan.

Chef's Note

The Ministry of Magic recommends all young witches and wizards to eat 7 portions of fruit and vegetables a day - and this vitamin-packed pasta is an easy way to get them in. '7, not 5?', we hear you ask. Yes, because 7 is the magic number. Muggles will catch on soon.

BELLATRIX LESTRANGE'S LASAGNE

SERVES 6

 Ingredients

- 2tbsp olive oil
- 800g/1 ¾lb beef mince
- 800g/1 ¾lb passata
- 200ml/7fl oz beef stock
- 1tsp grated nutmeg
- 300g/11oz fresh lasagne sheets
- 450ml/15 ½fl oz whole milk
- 50g/2oz butter
- 50g/2oz plain flour
- 125g/4oz mozzarella

Method

1 Heat the oil in a large frying pan and cook the beef for 10-15 minutes, until browned.

2 Add the passata and beef stock. Bring to the boil and simmer for 30 minutes.

3 Pre-heat the oven to 180°C/350°F/Gas Mark 4.

4 Make the white sauce by melting the butter in a small cauldron and then stirring in the flour to create the roux. Stir in a small amount of milk to make a paste. Keep adding the rest of the milk gradually, stirring continuously to ensure no lumps form. Heat gently for 5 minutes, until smooth.

5 Lightly grease a large, ovenproof dish, then spoon in a layer of the mince sauce, followed by a layer of lasagne sheets and one third of the white sauce. Repeat 2 more times.

6 Place the mozzarella on top and bake in the oven for 45 minutes, until bubbling. Serve while it's hot and menacing, like Bellatrix herself!

Chef's Note

This tasty lasagne is best enjoyed with garlic bread and salad. It is named after Bellatrix Lestrange, quite simply because it is fatal – once you've made it once, you'll want to make it again, and again, and again... Until one day, you fall through a curtain, and that's the end of it.

SEVERUS SNAPE'S SNAKE-Y BOLOGNESE

SERVES 4

Ingredients

- 1 tbsp olive oil
- 1 onion
- 2 cloves garlic
- 500g/1lb 2oz mince beef
- 100g/3½oz mushrooms, sliced
- 1 tsp mixed herbs
- 300ml/10½floz beef stock
- 400g/14oz chopped tomatoes
- 1 tbsp tomato ketchup
- 1 tbsp Worcestershire sauce
- Salt & black pepper
- 400g/14oz spaghetti
- Parmesan, grated

Method

1 Heat the oil in a large frying pan and cook the onion, garlic and mince, until brown.

2 Add the mushrooms and mixed herbs, and cook for a further few minutes.

3 Stir in the beef stock, chopped tomatoes, ketchup, Worcestershire sauce and a pinch of salt and pepper. Bring to the boil, then simmer for 30 minutes.

4 Meanwhile, cook the spaghetti snakes by bringing a large cauldron of water to the boil, and simmering for 10 minutes.

5 Drain and serve in bowls with the meat sauce ladled over the top, and a generous sprinkling of parmesan cheese.

Chef's Note

Back in their student days, Severus Snape used to daydream of the day he'd cook this delicious serpentine meal for his beloved Lily - after he'd strangled his arch-nemesis James Potter with a single strand of spaghetti, and humiliated him in front of the whole school. Ah, memories.

Firebolt Fajitas

SERVES 4

 Ingredients

- 3 chicken breasts, sliced
- 1 red onion, finely sliced
- 1 red pepper, deseeded and finely sliced
- 1 red chilli pepper, finely sliced
- 1 tbsp smoked paprika
- 1 tbsp coriander

- ½ tsp cumin
- 1tbsp olive oil
- Juice of 1 lime
- ¼ tsp tabasco
- 8 tortillas
- Iceberg lettuce
- Hot salsa
- Cheddar cheese

Method

1 In a large bowl, combine the chicken, onion, pepper and chilli with the paprika, coriander, cumin, olive oil, lime juice and tabasco. Leave to stand for 30 minutes to marinate.

2 Heat a large griddle pan on a high heat. Add the marinated chicken and vegetables, and sear. Turn the chicken pieces regularly, and stop once all the chicken appears cooked and charred – to test, break one piece of chicken in half and check cooked through. Or use magic, just to be sure.

3 Heat the tortillas in the microwave for 20 seconds.

4 Serve the tortillas and chicken hot, and dress with the lettuce, salsa and cheese.

Chef's Note

Firebolt Fajitas are so-called because of their hot and spicy flavour, which hits you like a Beater smashing a Bludger, and catches in the back of your throat, like a Seeker grasping at the Snitch. Harry Potter likes this dinner because it reminds him of his favourite ever broomstick (don't tell the Nimbus!)

Privet Drive Parmesan Chicken & Potatoes

SERVES 4

Ingredients

- 1 egg
- 4 chicken breasts
- 6 tbsp parmesan cheese, grated
- 400g/14oz new potatoes, halved
- 165g/5½oz frozen peas
- Salt & black pepper

Method

1 Pre-heat the grill to medium-high.

2 Separate the egg white into a bowl, and beat.

3 Lay each chicken breast in the bowl, and coat in egg white. Try to stop Dudley from eating the raw chicken by bribing him with chocolate.

4 Sprinkle grated parmesan over each chicken breast, then place on a pre-greased tray. Grill for 12 minutes, turning the chicken once, until it is cooked through.

5 Meanwhile, bring a cauldron of water to the boil. Cook the potatoes for 10 mins, adding the peas for the final 3 minutes.

6 Plate each chicken breast with a quarter of the vegetables, season with salt and pepper, and serve.

Chef's Note

This is a common weeknight dinner at No.4 Privet Drive, made by Aunt Petunia - it will probably not surprise you to learn, Vernon Dursley is a meat-and-two-veg kind of guy. Harry, of course, was served a much smaller portion, delivered through a cat-flap to his cupboard under the stairs.

YULE MEAT BALLS

SERVES 6

 Ingredients

- 5 tbsp olive oil
- 2 clove garlic, finely chopped
- 300g/10oz onion, finely chopped
- 900g/2lb minced beef
- 2 tbsp mixed herbs
- 1 egg, beaten

- Salt & black pepper
- 800g/1 ¾ lb tinned chopped tomatoes
- 1 tsp sugar
- 150g/5oz fresh mozzarella, grated
- 600g/1lb 5oz fresh tagliatelle

Method

1 Heat half of the olive oil in a small cauldron over a medium heat. Add half the garlic and half the onion, and cook until soft. Remove from heat and allow to cool.

2 In another cauldron, mix the minced beef with the cooked onion and garlic. Stir in the mixed herbs and beaten egg, and season with salt and pepper. Divide the mince mixture into 20-24 meat balls, then place in the fridge to cool.

3 Meanwhile, heat the remaining oil on a medium heat in another cauldron (you will need a lot of cauldrons for this dish!) Add the remaining onion and garlic, and cook until soft. Pour in the tinned tomatoes and sugar, a pinch of salt and pepper, and stir.

4 Leave the sauce to simmer on a low heat for approximately 30 minutes.

5 Meanwhile, heat a little more oil in a large cauldron (the flat, frying kind), over a medium-high heat, and cook the meatballs for approximately 10 minutes each.

6 Whilst they are cooking, bring (yet another!) cauldron of water to the boil, and cook the tagliatelle for 10 minutes, until al dente.

7 Pre-heat the grill.

8 Grease an ovenproof dish. Layer the cooked meatballs, then the tomato sauce, and top with the mozzarella. Place under the grill until the cheese is melted and bubbling.

9 Drain the tagliatelle, and serve with the mozzarella-coated meatballs. Mmmm.

52

PAN-COOKED PRAWN PATRONUS

SERVES 6

Ingredients

- 900g/2lb whole, shell-on prawns
- 2tbsp butter
- 1 tsp vegetable oil
- 1 tsp salt
- 2 cloves garlic, minced
- 1 tsp chilli flakes
- 1 lemon, quartered

Method

1 De-vein the prawns by using a sharp knife to score down the back of each prawn, and removing the thin digestive tract.

2 Rinse the prawns with water, and allow to dry on kitchen paper.

3 Heat the butter, oil and salt in a large cauldron on a high heat. Add the garlic, chilli and prawns, and cook for approximately 4 minutes, until the prawns are as pink as Dolores Umbridge's cardigan.

4 Serve immediately, with the lemon on the side to squeeze over.

Chef's Note

This seafood dish is named after a wizarding legend. It is said that many years ago, a young witch, faced with the horror of a dementor, summoned the last of her strength, clutched her wand, and yelled 'Expecto Patronum' - only to produce... a tiny prawn! Even more surprisingly, the fact that she lived to tell the tail suggests it must have worked.

Cedric Diggory's Stir-Fried Duck

SERVES 4

 Ingredients

- 275g/10oz jasmine rice
- 4 tbsp dark soy sauce
- 2 tbsp honey
- 4 duck breasts, sliced
- 1 tbsp vegetable oil
- 2 carrots, sliced
- 125g/4oz spring onions, sliced
- 1 small Chinese leaf cabbage, shredded

Method

1 Boil water in a large cauldron and cook the rice according to packet instructions.

2 In a bowl, mix the soy sauce and honey. Lay the slices of duck breast in to coat, then set aside.

3 Heat the oil in a large 'wok-like' cauldron. Stir-fry the duck on a high heat for 2 minutes. Add the carrot, spring onion and Chinese leaf, and pour in the left-over soy sauce and honey marinade. Stir-fry all ingredients for a further 3 minutes.

4 Drain the jasmine rice, and serve with the stir-fried duck and vegetables. Eat with chopsticks (or two wands) if you can!

Chef's Note

Cedric once cooked this delicious meal, his signature dish, for love interest Cho Chang. She liked it so much, she insisted he gave her the recipe – and thus, we are able to pass on the secret, even after Cedric's premature demise, allowing his true legacy to live on.

GOBLET OF FIRE JAMBALAYA

SERVES 8

Ingredients

- 450g/1lb andouille sausage, sliced
- 2 tbsp vegetable oil
- 1 large onion, chopped
- 4 sticks celery, chopped
- 1 red bell pepper, deseeded and chopped
- 4 garlic cloves, finely chopped
- 2 bay leaves

- 1 tsp paprika
- ½ tsp cayenne pepper
- 1 tsp dried thyme
- 1 tsp dried oregano
- 2 red chillies, deseeded and finely chopped
- 800g/1¾ lb tinned chopped tomatoes
- 750ml/1¼ pint chicken stock

- 350g/12oz uncooked rice
- 450g/1lb cooked chicken, shredded
- 450g/1lb medium prawns, deveined
- 1 handful fresh parsley, chopped
- Salt & black pepper

Method

1 Heat a large cauldron over a medium-high heat and cook the sliced sausage for 5 minutes, until browned. Remove and set aside.

2 In the same cauldron, mix the onion, celery, pepper, garlic, bay leaves, paprika, cayenne pepper, thyme and oregano and sauté for 5 minutes.

3 Add the chillies, tomatoes, chicken stock, rice, chicken and cooked sausage. Bring to the boil, then cover and simmer for 20 minutes, until rice is cooked.

4 Add the prawns, stir, and cook for a further 4-5 minutes, until the prawns are pink.

5 Serve immediately, sprinkled with the fresh parsley.

Chef's Note

The Goblet of Fire Jambalaya was so named because it's hot, fiery and made up of a jumble of ingredients – of which, 3 emerge over the others: chicken, sausage and prawn. Harry Potter is the parsley in this recipe – fresh-faced, green around the gills, and added last, whether he likes it or not!

Mad Eye Moody's Mac & Cheese

SERVES 4

 Ingredients

- 300g/11oz macaroni
- 75g/3oz butter
- 1 garlic clove, finely chopped
- 1tsp English mustard powder
- 3 tbsp plain flour
- 750ml/1¼ pint milk

- 50g/2oz parmesan cheese, grated
- 275g/10oz mature cheddar cheese, grated
- 50g/2oz breadcrumbs

 Method

1 Pre-heat the oven to 180°C/350°F/Gas Mark 4.

2 Bring a large cauldron of water to the boil, and cook the macaroni according to the packet instructions.

3 In another cauldron, melt 50g/2oz of the butter over a medium heat. Add the garlic and mustard powder, and cook for 1 minute.

4 Stir in the flour, to make a roux. Gradually add the milk, stirring continuously to avoid lumps.

5 Turn the heat to low, and add the cheddar and parmesan. Stir and simmer until the cheese has melted into the sauce.

6 In a large baking dish, layer the macaroni and pour the cheese sauce on top.

7 Sprinkle with the breadcrumbs, then bake for 25-30 minutes, until golden. Serve immediately.

Chef's Note

With an eye in the back of his head, Mad Eye was usually able to prepare his favourite mac 'n' cheese whilst simultaneously keeping an eye on dark wizards - until that is, the fateful day that Barty Crouch Jnr. came to kidnap him, when he'd unfortunately ran out of parmesan, and was thus distracted.

Voldemort's Vegan Burgers

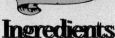

Ingredients

- 400g/14oz tin of chickpeas, drained
- 350/12oz tin of sweetcorn, drained
- 1 tsp dried coriander
- ½ tsp paprika
- ½ tsp cumin
- 3 tbsp plain flour
- 1 lemon
- 1 tbsp olive oil
- 4 large lettuce leaves
- 2 large tomatoes
- 4 tbsp tomato ketchup
- 4 wholemeal buns

Method

1 Put the drained chickpeas, sweetcorn, coriander, paprika, cumin and flour in a food processor. Grate the lemon zest, and add this too.

2 Pulse in the food processor until roughly blended. You're looking for the consistency of Muggle brains after Voldemort's finished with them.

3 Divide the mixture into 4 burger patties, and cool in the fridge for 20 minutes.

4 Heat the oil in a large, flat cauldron, and cook the burgers on a medium heat for 10 minutes, turning half-way through.

5 Layer each bun with a lettuce leaf, a burger and a dollop of tomato ketchup – and enjoy!

Chef's Note

Of course, Voldemort would never have eaten a vegan burger by choice – the complete lack of any torture, murder or unicorn blood involved in the process of its creation would have repulsed him – and so in lies the irony behind this delicious dish. If for no other reason, make these burgers to annoy Voldemort!

THE BURROW BLACK BEAN BURRITOS

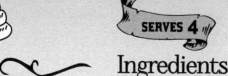

SERVES 4

Ingredients

- 4 tortillas
- 4 tbsp vegetable oil
- 1 red bell pepper, chopped
- 2 cloves garlic, finely chopped
- 1 jalapeño pepper, finely chopped
- 2 x 400g/14oz tins of black beans, drained
- 2 onions, chopped
- 175g/6oz Cheddar cheese, cubed
- 4 tbsp fresh coriander, chopped
- Guacamole
- Salsa

Method

1 Heat the oil in a large cauldron over medium heat. Cook the onion, pepper, garlic and jalapeño for 2 minutes.

2 Add the black beans, and cook for a further 3 minutes.

3 Stir the cheese and coriander into the beans and vegetable mix, and cook for 2 minutes.

4 Microwave the tortillas for 10 seconds each to warm (or use the Incendio spell).

5 Place a line of the bean mixture down each tortilla, and roll to form the burrito. Serve with the salsa and guacamole.

Chef's Note

With so many mouths to feed, the Weasleys often had to make 3 or 4 batches of these tasty burritos – especially when Harry and Hermione came to stay. Teenage wizards are like bottomless pits! It's a good job they had magic to help them.

SPINELESS LOCKHART'S CANNELLONI

SERVES 6

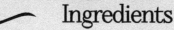

Ingredients

- 400g/14oz spinach
- 2 tsp olive oil
- ¼ tsp ground nutmeg
- 1 onion, finely chopped
- 2 cloves garlic, crushed
- 2 x 400g/14oz tins of chopped tomatoes
- 1 bay leaf

- Handful basil leaves
- Salt & black pepper
- 250g ricotta
- 1 egg, beaten
- 2 tsp parmesan, grated
- 150g cannelloni
- 250g mozzarella, sliced

Method

1 Pre-heat the oven to 180°C/350°F/Gas 4.

2 Heat 1 tsp of the oil in a cauldron over a medium heat. Add the spinach and nutmeg, and sauté until the spinach has wilted. Set aside in a bowl.

3 In the same cauldron, heat the 2nd tsp of oil, and cook the onion until soft. Add the garlic, chopped tomatoes, bay leaf and half the basil leaves. Season and simmer for 20 minutes. Practice artfully flicking your golden locks and telling a heroic-sounding story whilst you wait.

4 If you can drag yourself away from the mirror, add the ricotta, egg and parmesan to the bowl with the spinach, and mix well.

5 Stuff each cannelloni with the spinach and ricotta & lay in an oven-proof dish.

6 Pour the tomato sauce over the cannelloni, then layer the remaining basil leaves and sliced mozzarella on top. Bake in the oven for 35 mins, or until the cheese is golden.

Chef's Note

This is the kind of dish you'd expect Gilderoy Lockhart to love – it's safe, comforting & easy to make, yet looks & tastes like you've put far more effort in than you actually have. Of course, Lockhart wasn't the original creator of this recipe, but that's nothing a quick memory charm can't fix!

ROWENA RAVENCLAW'S RISOTTO

SERVES 4

Ingredients

- 100g/3½oz butter
- 400g/14oz assorted mushrooms, sliced
- 1 shallot, chopped
- 1 clove garlic, finely chopped
- 250g/9oz Arborio risotto rice
- 100ml/3½fl oz white wine
- 750ml/1¼ pint vegetable stock
- 1 tbsp truffle oil
- 50g/2oz parmesan, grated
- Salt & black pepper

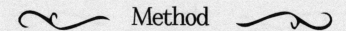

Method

1 Heat half of the butter in a large cauldron, and cook the mushrooms, shallots and garlic until soft.

2 Add the rice, and stir until clear (think Nearly Headless Nick).

3 Stir in the white wine, then add the vegetable stock slowly, a little at a time, until it has all been absorbed and the rice is cooked. This should take 15-20 minutes.

4 Add the truffle oil and remaining butter. Season with salt and pepper, stir in the parmesan, and serve.

Chef's Note

Originally from Scotland, Rowena Ravenclaw used to make this warming risotto on a cold winter's night in the glens, prior to founding the best wizarding school in the world. Perhaps this risotto was one of the keys to her success? Either way, it's best enjoyed with garlic bread and Chardonnay.

Lily Potter's Potato & Lentil Hotpot

SERVES 4

 ## Ingredients

- 600g/1lb 5oz potatoes, peeled and sliced
- 2 large onions, sliced
- 200g/7oz red lentils, washed
- 2 tsp Marmite

- 135ml/4½floz vegetable stock
- 40g/1½oz margarine
- Salt & black pepper

Method

1 Pre-heat the oven to 180°C/350°F/Gas Mark 4.

2 Grease a large pie dish. Add layers of the chopped potato, onions and lentils, finishing on a layer of potato.

3 Pour the vegetable stock over the dish, and dot with the margarine.

4 Cover the dish, and bake for 1 hour. Remove the lid for the last few minutes if you want a crunchy topping (this was James's favourite bit!)

Chef's Note

Rumour has it, Lily Potter was cooking this for her family the night that Voldemort arrived in Godric's Hollow to murder Harry. By the time Hagrid arrived to remove Harry from the rubble, James and Lily Potter were dead, and the hotpot was ruined. It was a bad night all round.

GODRIC GRYFFINDOR'S GRATIN

SERVES 4

Ingredients

- 2 tbsp olive oil
- 1 onion, chopped
- 2 cloves garlic, chopped
- 3 rashers bacon, sliced
- 1kg/2¼lb baking potatoes, peeled and sliced

- 300ml/10½fl oz milk
- 100ml/3½fl oz single cream
- 60g/ 2 ½ oz cheddar cheese, grated
- Salt & black pepper

Method

1 Pre-heat the oven to 180°C/350°F/Gas Mark 4.

2 Heat 1 tbsp oil in a large cauldron over a medium heat. Cook the onion and garlic until soft. Add the bacon and fry for 5 minutes. Remove from heat, drain and place in a pre-greased baking dish.

3 Add the potatoes and milk to the dish with the onion, garlic and bacon. Season with salt and pepper, and mix.

4 Pour over the cream and Gruyere cheese, and bake for 40 minutes, until golden – like a Gryffindor lion.

Chef's Note

This dish is brave, chivalrous and sometimes cheesy, just like Godric Gryffind or himself was rumoured to be. He loved a good pun, did Godric – he often enjoyed one with his old friend, Salazar Slytherin, before they fell out over the whole muggle-born thing.

RITA SKEETER'S SWEET POTATO CURRY

SERVES 2

Ingredients

- 2 tbsp olive oil
- 1 onion, chopped
- 1 tbsp red curry paste
- 1 tsp mustard seeds
- 100g/3½oz red lentils
- 2 sweet potatoes, peeled and chopped

- 450ml/15½ fl oz vegetable stock
- 400g/14oz chopped tomatoes
- 400g/14oz tin chickpeas, drained
- 2 naan breads
- Jasmine rice, cooked, to serve

Method

1 Heat the oil in a large cauldron on a medium heat. Add the onion, curry paste and mustard seeds, and cook until the onion is soft.

2 Add the lentils, sweet potato, vegetable stock and chopped tomatoes. Bring to the boil, then simmer for 20 minutes, until the lentils are cooked.

3 Stir in the chickpeas, and heat for a further 5 minutes.

4 Serve hot, with the naan breads and cooked rice.

Chef's Note

Rita Skeeter likes to make this quick Sweet Potato Curry for her one-on-one interviews, for the sole reason that the strong flavour disguises the subtle taste of Veritaserum. She serves it with naan bread, on a bed of lies – rice, we mean rice.

Sybil Trelawney's Tofu Stir Fry

SERVES 4

Ingredients

- 2 tbsp vegetable oil
- 350g/12oz tofu
- 1 head broccoli, divided into florets
- 4 garlic cloves, chopped
- 1 red chilli, deseeded and chopped
- 125g/4oz spring onions, sliced
- 2 heads pak choi, chopped
- 140g/4½oz soya beans
- 1 tbsp soy sauce
- ½ lime
- 25g/1oz cashew nuts

Method

1 Cut the tofu into cubes, and drain thoroughly using kitchen paper.

2 Heat 1 tbsp oil over a medium heat in a large wok-shaped cauldron, and fry the tofu pieces for 6-8 minutes, or until golden. Remove to kitchen paper to drain.

3 Heat the remaining oil in the wok, and stir fry the broccoli florets for 5 minutes. Add the garlic, chilli, spring onions, soy beans and pak choi, and fry for 3-4 minutes.

4 Stir in the soy sauce, juice from the lime, cashew nuts and fried tofu, and heat through for 30 seconds. Divide into bowls (or teacups, if wanting to read fortunes later), and serve immediately.

Chef's Note

The Professor of Divination might be known for being a bit 'out there', but this Tofu Stir Fry is surprisingly ok. You can even have a Prophecy half way through, and the worst that will happen is the tofu gets a bit soggy, or the broccoli catches - oh, and maybe a wizarding family gets ripped apart.

Spellbinding Spanish Tortilla

SERVES 4

Ingredients

- 500g/1lb 2oz potatoes, peeled and sliced
- 1 onion, chopped
- 6 eggs
- 150ml/5fl oz olive oil
- Salt & black pepper

Method

1 In a bowl, combine the potato and onion.

2 In a large, non-stick cauldron, heat the olive oil on a medium heat. Add the potato and onion, and leave to cook slowly for 30 minutes, or until the potatoes are cooked. If they start to burn, reduce the heat. Once cooked, remove from the cauldron and strain in a colander.

3 Beat the eggs in a large bowl, then mix in the onion and potato. Stir to coat.

4 Heat a little more oil (or the strained oil from earlier) in a large non-stick cauldron.

5 Pour the mixture into the cauldron, flatten and leave to cook for 20 minutes. Once the base is brown and the tortilla is almost set, place a dinner plate over the top, turn the omelette out onto it, then use the spatula to slide the tortilla back into the pan, the other way up (or just use magic!)

6 Cook for a further 3-4 minutes, until the new underside is also browned.

7 Slide onto a plate and allow to cool for 5 minutes before serving. Delicious hot or cold!

Chef's Note

This Spellbinding Spanish Tortilla is a magical delicacy, often enjoyed by witches and wizards on holiday.

BEATER BUDDHA BOWL

SERVES 4

 Ingredients

- 1 cup quinoa
- 1 sweet potato, cut into chunks
- 1 tsp olive oil
- 400g/14oz tin of chickpeas, drained
- 3 tsp maple syrup
- 1½ tsp chilli powder

- ½ tsp paprika
- ½ tsp garlic powder
- 1 cup red cabbage, chopped
- 1 cup spinach
- 4 tbsp tahini
- ½ tsp turmeric
- Salt & black pepper
- 1 avocado, sliced

 Method

1 Pre-heat the oven to 180°C/350°F/Gas 4.

2 Lay the sweet potato chunks on a baking tray, and drizzle with olive oil. Bake in the oven for 35 minutes, until cooked.

3 Cook the quinoa by bringing 2 cups of water to boil in a large cauldron, then adding the quinoa and simmering for 15 minutes. Remove from heat and set aside.

4 In a bowl, combine the chickpeas, 2 tsp maple syrup, 1 tsp chilli powder, paprika and garlic powder. Stir to ensure the chickpeas are coated.

5 Heat a cauldron (pewter is best) over a medium heat, and cook the chickpeas for 10 mins, stirring continuously, until sticky.

6 In a separate cauldron, wilt first the red cabbage, then the spinach, over a low heat.

7 Make the dressing by mixing the tahini with the turmeric, the remaining maple syrup and chilli powder, and 4 tbsp of warm water. Season with salt and pepper.

8 To assemble the Buddha Bowl, layer the cooked quinoa in the bottom of a large bowl, then add the sweet potato chunks, chickpeas, spinach, red cabbage and sliced avocado. Drizzle with the tahini dressing, and serve to a nervous, pre-match Beater!

Chef's Note

Beaters are known to consume this protein packed meal before a Quidditch match.

Blue Cheese Stuffed Beater-nut Squash

SERVES 2

Ingredients

- 1 large butternut squash
- 1 clove garlic, finely chopped
- 50g/2oz butter
- Salt & black pepper
- 1 tsp olive oil
- 75g/3oz walnuts, toasted and chopped
- 200g/7oz blue cheese
- 1 tbsp honey

Method

1 Pre-heat the oven to 190°C /375°F/Gas Mark 5.

2 Cut the squash in half lengthwise and scoop out the seeds.

3 Add the chopped garlic and butter to each half. Season with salt and pepper, brush with oil, and roast in the oven for 1 hour, or until the flesh is soft.

4 Scoop the flesh out into a bowl. Mash the flesh, and mix in the blue cheese and walnuts.

5 Spoon the filling back into the squash halves, drizzle the honey on top, and cook for a further 15 minutes. Serve 1 squash half to each ravenous Beater, with salad.

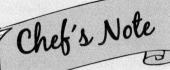

Chef's Note

After all that Bludger-beating is done, Beaters like to celebrate with a stuffed beater-nut squash. After a particularly bad match against Slytherin, it is rumoured that rebellious Gryffindor Beaters Fred & George Weasley once removed the stuffing, and filled it with Ogden's Old Firewhisky instead!

Ron Weasley's Really Good Wellington

SERVES 6

Ingredients

- 2 tsp vegetable oil
- 650g/1lb 7oz fillet of dragon (beef)
- 25g/1oz butter
- 500g/1lb 2oz chestnut mushrooms, chopped
- 1 spring fresh thyme
- 100ml dry white wine
- 6 slices prosciutto
- 500g puff pastry
- Plain flour, for dusting
- 1 egg, beaten

Method

1 Heat the oil in a large pan. Sear the meat for 30 seconds on each side.

2 Heat the butter in a large cauldron. Add the chestnut mushrooms and thyme, and cook for 15 minutes, until golden. Pour in the dry white wine, and cook for a further 10 minutes, until the wine is absorbed. Remove from heat and leave to cool.

3 Place clingfilm on your worktop. Place the slices of prosciutto on top, overlapping to form a sheet. Layer ¾ of the mushrooms, then the beef, and the remaining mushrooms. Use the clingfilm to wrap the beef and mushrooms tightly in the prosciutto, then chill for 10 minutes.

4 On a floured surface, roll out the puff pastry into a 35cm square. Remove the clingfilm from the dragon, place in the centre of the pastry, and wrap the pastry around the meat, using the beaten egg to seal. Fold in all the edges, and seal. Use the blunt end of a knife to score shallow ridges in the top of the wellington, then brush all over with the beaten egg and chill for 30 minutes.

5 Pre-heat the oven to 230°C/450°F/Gas Mark 8.

6 Cook the wellington in the oven for 10 minutes, then reduce the heat to 200°C/400°F/Gas Mark 6, and cook for a further 20 minutes.

7 Remove the wellington from the oven and leave to cool for 10 minutes. Serve sliced, with a red wine sauce and vegetables.

Diagon Alley Ale Pie

Ingredients

- 900g/2lb steak, diced
- 25g/1oz flour
- 50g/2oz butter
- 2 onions, chopped
- 2 cloves garlic, chopped
- 2 carrots, chopped
- 1 sprig fresh thyme

- 400ml/14 fl oz ale
- 450ml/15½ fl oz beef stock
- Salt & black pepper
- 1 egg, beaten
- 900g/2lb ready-made puff pastry

Method

1 Put the meat and flour in a bowl, and stir to coat. Heat the butter in a cauldron, and sear the floured meat until golden.

2 Add the onions, garlic, carrots, thyme, ale and beef stock. Season with salt and pepper. Cover and simmer for 1 hour, until cooked.

3 Pre-heat the oven to 220°C/425°F/Gas Mark 7.

4 Grease a large pie dish. Take two thirds of the puff pastry and roll it out flat, then use to line the pie dish.

5 Add the filling to the pie. Brush the edges of the pastry in the dish with the beaten egg, then roll the remaining third of the pastry, and place on top to make the lid.

6 Trim and crimp the edges of the pie, using any leftovers to decorate the top. Brush the top thoroughly with the beaten egg.

7 Make a couple of slits in the top of the pie with a knife, then bake in the oven for 30-40 minutes, until golden, and ready to serve to hungry wizards!

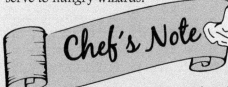

Chef's Note

This pie is served in the Leaky Cauldron to tired witches and wizards after a long day shopping in Diagon Alley. It usually comes with pea and carrots, and is very reasonably priced – much appreciated by parents who have been coerced into buying their offspring the latest designer dress robes.

Quirrell's Quesadilla

SERVES 4

Ingredients

- 2 tbsp olive oil
- 2 cloves garlic, finely chopped
- 225g/8oz mushrooms, chopped
- 225g/8oz spinach, chopped
- Salt & black pepper
- 2 cups brie cheese, cubed
- 8 flour tortillas

Method

1 Heat 1 tbsp of the olive oil in a cauldron over a medium heat. Add the garlic and mushrooms, and cook for 5-6 minutes, until the mushrooms are golden. Daydream about finding the Philosopher's Stone whilst you wait.

2 Stir in the spinach and cook for 2 more minutes, until the spinach is wilted. Season with salt and pepper.

3 Pre-heat the oven to 200°C/400°F/Gas Mark 6.

4 Brush 1 side of each of the tortillas with the remaining olive oil.

5 On a baking tray, place a tortilla oil side down, then layer some spinach and mushrooms, and a quarter of the brie cubes.

Top with another tortilla, oil side up. Repeat 3 more times, until all the tortillas and filling has been used.

6 Bake for 10 minutes, turning once halfway through, until the tortillas are golden.

Chef's Note

This crafty Quesadilla is named after Professor Quirrell, because it's flat, beige and moon-like - like the Voldemort, living in the back of your head. If you use unicorn blood instead of brie, it can keep you alive, even if you are moments from death - but at a terrible price.

DECREE

DUMBLEDORE'S JUMBLE CRUMBLE

SERVES 4

Ingredients

- 225g/8oz plain flour
- 110g/3½oz unsalted butter (diced)
- 75g/3oz caster sugar

- 2 tablespoons sugar
- 700g/1lb 9oz fresh or frozen mixed summer berries

Method

1 Pre-heat the oven to 180°C/350°F/Gas Mark 4.

2 To make the topping, sieve the flour into a large mixing bowl, then add the butter and rub it in, until it forms a breadcrumb-like consistency. Add the caster sugar, and mix it in.

3 Pour the mixed berries into an oven-proof baking dish. Sprinkle the sugar on top, then add the crumble mixture and press it down firmly with a fork.

4 Bake the crumble in the oven for approx. 30 minutes, until it's golden and good enough for Albus Dumbledore himself!

Chef's Note

This delicious, buttery crumble is widely believed to have been the beloved Hogwarts headmaster's favourite tea-time treat. According to the updated Chocolate Frog card, his preferred flavour was raspberry and wolfsbane, and he enjoyed it with hot custard.

CORNELIUS FUDGE CAKE

SERVES 8

 Ingredients

- 175g/6oz self-raising flour
- 5 tbsp cocoa powder
- 1 tsp bicarbonate soda
- 150g/5oz caster sugar
- 2 eggs, beaten

- 150ml/5floz vegetable oil
- 150ml/5floz semi-skimmed milk
- 2 tbsp golden syrup
- 75g/3oz butter
- 175g/6oz icing sugar

Method

1 Pre-heat the oven to 180°C/350°F/Gas Mark 4.

2 Grease 2 baking tins. In a bowl, mix the flour, 2 tbsp cocoa powder, bicarbonate soda and sugar.

3 Put the eggs, oil, milk and syrup in a separate bowl, and mix well using a stirring charm (or electric whisk, if Muggle). Make a well in the centre of the flour, and mix the liquid into the flour.

4 Pour the mixture into the 2 tins, and bake for 25 minutes, until firm. Turn out onto wire racks to cool.

5 In a bowl, mix the butter, icing sugar and remaining 3 tbsp cocoa powder, to make the butter icing. If needed, add

a drop of water to make smoother. Keep away from hungry Ministers for Magic, in case of premature consumption.

6 Sandwich the 2 cake halves together with butter icing, then cover the whole cake with the remaining butter icing.

Chef's Note

When Cornelius Fudge was Minister for Magic and received the news that Voldemort had returned, instead of listening to the evidence and witnesses, and taking action that could have potentially saved lives, he chose denial – and to bury his head in a large plate of this Chocolate Fudge Cake. Nice.

Seamus Finnigan's Fruit Salad

SERVES 4

Ingredients

- 1 pink grapefruit
- 1 orange
- 60ml/2fl oz water
- 100g/3½oz sugar
- 1 lemongrass stalk
- 1 lime

- 1 cup strawberries
- 1 cup cherries
- 1 apple, sliced
- 1 pear, sliced
- 1 kiwi, sliced

Method

1 Chop the grapefruit and orange into segments. Preserve the citrus juice.

2 Heat the citrus juice, water and sugar in a small cauldron, until the sugar dissolves. Add the lemongrass, and a strip of the lime skin, and bring to the boil, then simmer over a low heat for 10 minutes. Remove from heat and allow to cool.

3 Meanwhile, combine the chopped grapefruit, orange, strawberries, cherries, apple, pear and kiwi in a bowl. Pour in a splash of lime juice, and mix.

4 Serve the fruit salad in individual goblets, with the syrup poured over.

Chef's Note

It is said that Gryffindor student Seamus Finnigan made Harry Potter a goblet of his famous fruit salad (one of his Muggle father's recipes) to apologise for not initially believing him that Voldemort had returned. Harry would have forgiven him anyway, but the fruit salad definitely sweetened the deal!

CHARLIE WEASLEY'S CHEESECAKE

SERVES 1

 ## Ingredients

- 200g/7oz white chocolate
- 175g/6oz digestive biscuits
- 300g/11oz full fat cream cheese
- 50g/2oz butter, unsalted
- 300ml/10½floz double cream
- 1 tsp lemon juice
- 1 tsp vanilla extract

Method

1 Melt the white chocolate in a small bowl oven a cauldron filled with 2 inches of boiled water, on a low heat. Once melted, remove and set aside to cool.

2 Blend the biscuits in a food processor. Add the butter, and blend again.

3 Press the blended biscuit mix into the base of an 8inch baking tin, and leave in the fridge to cool.

4 Beat the cream cheese in a bowl, then fold in the melted white chocolate.

5 Whip the double cream until it thickens, then fold this into the white chocolate mix. Add the lemon juice and vanilla extract, and fold this in too.

6 Pour the topping into the biscuit-lined tins. Smooth the top, cover with clingfilm, and refrigerate overnight before serving (unless magical, in which case you can use the Glacius charm, and eat instantly – lucky witch!)

Chef's Note

Having lived mostly alone in Romania and other remote regions of the world whilst working with dragons, Charlie Weasley had a lot of time to himself, and became a pretty good cook. His White Chocolate Cheesecake is a particular speciality – and the dragons don't like it, which is a bonus!

CHAMBER OF SECRETS
CHOCOLATE SUNDAE

SERVES 4

Ingredients

- 1 x 400g/14oz can sweetened condensed milk
- 100g/3½oz dark cooking chocolate, broken

- 12 scoops vanilla ice cream
- 8 Bourbons, or other chocolate cream biscuit
- Handful hazelnuts, crushed

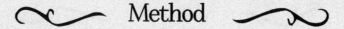

Method

1 Heat the condensed milk and cooking chocolate in a small cauldron over a low heat.

2 Stir continuously for 3 minutes, until the chocolate has melted. Remove from heat.

3 To assemble the sundaes, layer scoops of ice cream and chocolate sauce in 4 goblets (or less, if planning to face a Basilisk later).

4 Top with the crushed hazelnuts, and serve each sundae with a Bourbon biscuit.

Chef's Note

Years after Ginny Weasley was rescued from the Chamber of Secrets by Harry Potter, and the story had passed into legend, a wizarding café came up with this name for its new Chocolate Sundae. It went down a treat, of course. The magic folk love a good macabre reference with their food.

McGonagall's Black Forest Gateau

SERVES 8

Ingredients

- 125g/4oz caster sugar
- 125g/4oz butter
- 2 tbsp cocoa powder
- 2 eggs, beaten
- 125g/4oz self-raising flour
- 1 tbsp baking powder

- 2 tbsp milk
- 2 tsp caster sugar
- 175ml/6floz ml whipping cream
- 400g/14oz cherries in syrup
- Fresh cherries, to serve

Method

1 Pre-heat the oven to 180°C/350°F/Gas 4.

2 In a large bowl, cream together the 125g of sugar and butter.

3 Mix the cocoa with 3 tbsp of hot water, to form a chocolate paste.

4 Add the chocolate paste and beaten eggs to the sugar/butter mixture, and combine, then, sift in the flour and baking powder, and fold. Stir in the milk (keep away from cats).

5 Pour the cake mixture into a greased, 8inch baking tin. Bake for 30 minutes, or until cooked.

6 Turn the cake out of the tin, and leave to cool on a wire rack. Once cooled, slice the cake in half.

7 In another bowl, beat the 2 tsp sugar and whipping cream.

8 Spoon the whipped cream and half of the cherries onto one half of the cake to make the filling. Top with the other cake half, and arrange the remaining cherries on top. Serve with fresh cherries to garnish.

Chef's Note

Being an expert in Transfiguration means that Professor McGonagall can magic this gateau into existence from pretty much any vegetable or mineral. Muggles, and the less magical adept, can take the long road, follow this recipe, and hope for the best!

CRUCIO COOKIE DOUGH

SERVES 4

Ingredients

- 1 cup brown sugar
- ¼ cup granulated sugar
- 1 cup unsalted butter
- 1 tsp salt

- 1 tsp vanilla extract
- 2 cups flour
- 2 tbsp milk
- 1 cup chocolate chips

Method

1 Cream together the sugars and butter in a large vessel until fluffy. Use either an electric hand mixer, or a bewitched wooden spoon.

2 Beat in the salt and vanilla extract.

3 Mix in the flour, until crumbly.

4 Add the milk a little at a time, beating as you go, until this is also combined, and the dough starts to take shape.

5 Lastly, stir in the chocolate chips (you could also use Smarties, white chocolate chips, nuts, marshmallows, or any other Muggle treat you fancy), and it's ready to eat!

Chef's Note

So-called because it's so good, it's painful! As with other recipes with spells in the title, care must always be taken. The last thing you want is to accidentally perform the Cruciatus Curse on your dining companions, and find yourself locked up in Azkaban, whilst they all tuck into your share!

NOX CHOCOLATE PECAN CLUSTERS

SERVES 8

Ingredients

- 450g/1lb ripe sticky dates
- 1 cup coconut milk
- 1 tsp vanilla extract

- 125g/4oz pecan halves
- 225g/8oz Nox (dark) chocolate

Method

1 Using a food processor (or your choice of mixing spell), combine the sticky dates, coconut milk and vanilla extract.

2 Assemble your pecan clusters on a tray, by layering 2 or 3 pecan halves, then a layer of the date caramel, then more pecans. Refrigerate for 20 minutes to solidify.

3 Meanwhile, melt the Nox chocolate in a small bowl over a cauldron of recently boiled water, on a low heat.

4 Once cooled, remove the clusters from the fridge, drizzle over the melted chocolate, and serve.

Chef's Note

These easy pecan clusters are named after the darkness spell, Nox. This is both because they taste best when made with dark chocolate, and also because they are best enjoyed in the dead of night, as a cheeky midnight snack when the rest of the wizarding world is asleep!

Hogwarts Express Eton Mess

SERVES 4

Ingredients

- 400g/14oz strawberries
- 400ml/14floz double cream
- 1 tbsp caster sugar
- 4 meringue nests

Method

1 Take 100g of the strawberries and press through a sieve, to make a purée.

2 Whisk the cream and sugar together in a large bowl until it forms soft peaks (like the rolling hills seen from the windows of the Hogwarts Express).

3 Crumble the meringue nests, and fold into the whipped cream.

4 Slice the remaining strawberries, and fold these into the cream/meringue mixture.

5 Divide between 4 goblets, drizzle over the strawberry sauce, and serve immediately.

Chef's Note

Muggles like to enjoy their version of this dish whilst watching tennis at Wimbledon. For witches and wizards however, this is a classic travelling snack, to take with you in the flying car, on the train to Hogwarts, or even whilst apparating – the theory being, it's already a mess, so it can't get damaged in transit!

Voldemort's Venetian Ice Cream Cake

SERVES 4

Ingredients

- 1 litre/1½ pints coffee ice cream
- 175ml/6floz butterscotch sauce
- 100g/3½oz pecans, chopped
- 50g/2oz milk chocolate,

- 1 litre/1½ pints vanilla ice cream
- 250ml/8floz double cream, chilled
- ½ tbsp caster sugar
- ½ tbsp corn starch
- shaved

Method

1 Line a metal loaf tin with 2 layers of clingfilm, allowing some to extend over the edges.

2 Use a spatula to press ¼ of the coffee ice cream into the bottom of the tin. Drizzle with 1 tbsp butterscotch sauce, and 1 tbsp pecans.

3 Press ¼ of the vanilla ice cream on top, to form the next layer. Drizzle with 1 tbsp butterscotch sauce, and 1 tbsp pecans.

4 Freeze for 20 minutes. Repeat layering and freezing process 4 times.

5 Finally, cover the top with the clingfilm overhang, and freeze the whole cake for

4 hours. (Why not plot the mass murder of some Muggles while you wait?)

6 Meanwhile, whip the chilled double cream, sugar and corn starch in a large bowl, until it forms soft peaks.

7 To remove cake from tin, fold back the clingfilm lid. Use a warm damp towel to loosen it from the tin, then invert cake onto a plate, and remove the clingfilm.

8 Use a pastry bag to pipe the whipped cream on top of the cake. Freeze for 1 more hour, until topping is frozen.

9 Allow to stand at room temperature for 10 minutes. Sprinkle the chocolate shavings over the top, slice, and serve.

HUFFLE-PUFF PASTRY APPLE TART

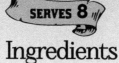

SERVES 8

Ingredients

- 375g/13oz all-butter puff pastry
- 5 large cooking apples
- Juice of 1 lemon

- 1 tbsp brown sugar
- 1 tbsp cinnamon
- 35g/1oz butter, cubed
- 3 tbsp maple syrup

Method

1 Pre-heat the oven to 220°C/425°F/Gas 7.

2 Line a baking tray with parchment paper. Roll out the pastry to a disc about 35cm across, and place on the baking tray.

3 Peel, core and slice the cooking apples. In a bowl, mix the apples and lemon juice.

4 Arrange the apple slices over the centre of the pastry disc, leaving a 2cm gap around the edges. Fold the edges up to make the sides of the tart.

5 Sprinkle over the brown sugar, cinnamon and cubes of butter.

6 Bake for 20 minutes, or until the pastry is crisp and golden. You should have no trouble waiting – Hufflepuffs are very patient.

7 Warm the maple syrup for 20 seconds in the microwave. Remove the tart from the oven and brush with the warmed maple syrup to glaze. Serve immediately.

Chef's Note

The Hufflepuff family are famous for 2 things: 1. Being related to one of the founders of Hogwarts, and 2. Their incredible puff pastry creations (did you realise that's where the name for puff pastry comes from?) Their delicious Apple Tart recipe is best enjoyed with vanilla ice cream.

CHOCOLATE BROWNIE IN A MUG-GLE

SERVES 1

Ingredients

- 2 tbsp butter
- 2 tbsp milk
- ¼ tsp vanilla extract
- 4 tbsp caster sugar
- 2 tbsp cocoa powder
- 4 tbsp plain flour

Method

1 Melt the butter in a mug in the microwave for a few seconds.

2 Whisk in the milk and vanilla extract using a fork.

3 Add the cocoa powder, sugar and flour, whisking in between each.

4 Microwave for 75 seconds (or a few seconds longer, if you want it less gooey).

5 Eat immediately!

Chef's Note

A tongue-in-cheek take on the popular Muggle 'Brownie in a Mug' cake, witches and wizards love using what Muggles call a 'microwave' to make this dessert – they find it fascinatingly quaint. It also makes a great cure, for the morning after one-too-many meads!

GOLDEN SNITCH SYRUP CAKE

SERVES 8

Ingredients

- 100g/3½oz brown sugar
- 200g /7oz butter
- 2 eggs

- 2 tbsp golden syrup
- 200g/7oz self-raising flour

Method

1 Pre-heat the oven to 170°C/325°F/Gas Mark 3.

2 In a bowl, beat together the brown sugar and butter.

3 In another bowl, whisk the eggs and golden syrup together, then add to the sugar/butter mix.

4 Fold in the flour, and mix until smooth.

5 Grease a small baking tin, and pour the cake mix in

6 Bake for 30 minutes. Brush up on your broom work whilst you wait.

7 Check cake is cooked by sliding a knife into the middle of the cake – if it comes out clean, it's ready to eat!

Chef's Note

This is the cake that every Seeker secretly wants on his or her birthday – combining delicious, syrupy cake with their dream of having the Golden Snitch in their possession. Ginny still makes this for Harry on the 31st of July, even now!

SORCERER'S

Snacks & Drinks

Hedwig's Hazelnut & Banana Toastie

SERVES 1

 Ingredients

- 150g/5oz hazelnuts
- 1 tablespoon honey
- 2 slices granary bread

- 1 banana
- ½ tsp cinnamon

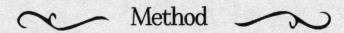 Method

1 Blend the hazelnuts in a food processor until they form a paste.

2 Drizzle in the honey, and mix further to make a smooth nut butter. Defend from owls.

3 Toast the bread, and slice the banana.

4 Layer the sliced banana on one slice of the toast, and dust with the cinnamon.

5 Spread the hazelnut butter on the other slice of toast, then sandwich together and eat immediately.

Chef's Note

Every owl needs a hearty breakfast before a long day of carrying post, parcels (and even broomsticks!) to eager Hogwarts students. Harry used to sneak these toasties into the Owlery for Hedwig, to make sure she had plenty of protein - essential for shiny feathers and speedy deliveries.

THE HALF BLOOD PRINCE'S POTION

 SERVES 1

Ingredients

- Ice cubes
- 1 tbsp sugar syrup
- 1 tbsp lemon juice
- 60ml/2floz Ogden's Old

- Firewhisky (or similar)
- 1 cherry, with stem
- 1 slice lemon peel, to garnish

Method

1 Fill a cocktail shaker with ice.

2 Pour in the sugar syrup, lemon juice and whisky, and shake well.

3 Serve in a goblet, over ice. Garnish with the cherry and lemon peel hooked over the side of the goblet.

4 Top tip: For an 'edgier' feel, try serving instead in a crystal phial!

Chef's Note

Severus Snape, a.k.a. The Half-Blood Prince, invented this cocktail whilst still at school, as a way to give himself the confidence to tell Lily how he felt – but he ended up drinking too much, and fell asleep. He awoke to a bad headache, and the news that Lily had been wooed by James Potter. Don't drink kids*.

*Seriously. This recipe is strictly for witches and wizards 'of-age'. That's 18 years +.

Lupin's Full Moon Party Mocktail

SERVES 1

Ingredients

- Ice cubes
- 60ml/2floz cranberry juice
- 25ml/1floz lime juice
- Juice from 1 orange
- 60ml/2floz lemonade
- 1 slice orange peel
- Sugar, to serve

Method

1 Fill a cocktail shaker with ice.

2 Pour in cranberry juice, lime juice and orange juice. Shake well to mix.

3 Add the lemonade, and stir (that's right – magical mocktails are shaken and stirred!)

4 Wet the rim of a goblet, and dip in sugar.

5 Pour in the mocktail, garnish with orange peel, and serve!

Chef's Note

Of course, Lupin would have preferred a 'proper' drink after a hard night of racing through the woods and howling at the moon - but alcohol isn't a good idea for Werewolves. Ever seen an angry drunk? Now imagine that drunk has claws, fangs and an uncontrollable desire to bite you... you see our point.

PHILOSOPHER'S STONE-LESS MARINATED OLIVES

SERVES 2

Ingredients

- 2 cups mixed olives, pitted
- 1 clove garlic, crushed
- ½ tbsp salt
- 1 tsp chilli flakes
- 1 tbsp dried oregano
- ½ cup olive oil
- ¼ cup red wine vinegar

Method

1 Drain the olives and place them in a lunch box (if you don't have one, ask Ron to borrow the one his mum uses for his corned beef sandwiches).

2 Add the garlic, salt, chilli, oregano, olive oil and vinegar.

3 Put the lid on the box, and shake vigorously to coat.

4 Serve immediately, or store in the fridge for later.

Chef's Note

Did you know? There is a wizarding restaurant that serves a set menu entirely dedicated to Harry Potter! It has 7 courses - 1 to represent each of Harry's years at Hogwarts. The menu kicks off with these Philosopher's Stone-less Olives, and culminates in a Deathly Hallows Dessert!

DEMENTOR-ED EGGS

SERVES 6

 Ingredients

- 6 eggs
- 2 tbsp mayonnaise
- ½ tsp salt

- ½ tsp pepper
- 1 tsp mustard
- 1 tbsp paprika

 Method

1 Hard boil the eggs in a cauldron of boiling water for 12 minutes.

2 Remove and place the eggs in cold water to cool.

3 Peel the shell off each egg and slice in half lengthways. Scoop out the yolks and place in a separate bowl.

4 Add the mayonnaise, salt, pepper and mustard to the yolks, and stir to mix. (You're looking for a creamy, 'soul-like' consistency. Mmmm).

5 Scoop the egg yolk mixture back into the centre of the egg whites.

6 Sprinkle with the paprika powder, and serve.

Chef's Note

This tasty recipe is a variation on the Muggle snack 'Devilled Eggs' - but as the name suggests, it's much more terrifying (not just because of the paprika!) In fact, these eggs are often served to convicted criminals as a last supper, before they receive the 'Dementor's Kiss' - a cruel yoke.

Dobby's Doughnuts

SERVES 10

 Ingredients

- 500g/1lb 2oz white flour
- 50g/2oz caster sugar
- 40g/1½oz butter
- 2 eggs
- 15g/½oz instant yeast
- 1 tsp salt
- 150ml/5floz milk
- 125ml/4floz water
- Caster sugar, for dusting
- 300g/11oz strawberry jam

Method

1 Place the flour, sugar, butter, eggs, yeast, salt, milk and water in a large bowl. Knead into a dough using your hands, or a mixer with dough hook, for 5 minutes.

2 Dust your surface with flour, tip the dough out, and knead for a further 10 minutes.

3 Place the dough in another bowl, cover with a tea towel, and leave to prove for 1 hour.

4 Tip the proved dough out onto a floured surface, knead briefly, and divide into 10 dough balls. Leave to rise for 1 hour.

5 Pre-heat a deep fat fryer filled with sunflower oil to 180°C/350°F.

6 Lower each doughnut into the fryer and cook for 10 minutes, turning halfway through, until golden.

7 Remove the doughnuts from the oil, and roll in caster sugar. Leave to cool completely.

8 Use a sharp knife to make a slit in each doughnut, and then use a piping bag or syringe to pipe jam into the middle of each one.

9 Serve to Harry Potter and the other house elves!

PATRONUS POPCORN

SERVES 4

Ingredients

- 2 tbsp coconut oil
- 75g/3oz popcorn kernels
- 50g/2oz butter

- 40g/1½oz brown sugar
- 2 tbsp golden syrup
- Salt

Method

1 Heat the oil in a large cauldron over a medium heat. Pour in the kernels, and stir to coat.

2 Cover the cauldron, turn the heat down low, and leave kernels to 'pop'. As soon as the frequency of popping noises starts to decrease, remove from the heat to avoid burning the popcorn.

3 In another cauldron, melt the butter over a high heat, then stir in the sugar and syrup, and heat for 1 minute. Add a pinch of salt.

4 Pour the toffee sauce into the cauldron of popcorn, cover and shake to coat.

5 Divide into 4 bowls, and serve. Bank this as a happy memory, in case you should need it in future.

Chef's Note

This toffee popcorn snack is named after the Patronus charm, because each batch is different, just as every Patronus is different. Make the snack last longer by seeing who can find the best animal-shaped popcorn piece – 10 bonus points for the best stag!

HIPPOGRIFF
MOZZARELLA STICKS

SERVES 1

Ingredients

- 450g/1lb Hippogriff mozzarella or buffalo mozzarella
- 1 cup flour
- 2 eggs, beaten
- 1 cup dry breadcrumbs
- 1 cup tomato ketchup or sundried tomato sauce

Method

1 Cut the mozzarella into 16 equally sized sticks, approx. 4 inches long.

2 Lay the mozzarella sticks in the flour to coat.

3 Dip each stick into the beaten egg, then roll in breadcrumbs.

4 Put the breadcrumb-coated sticks on a plate, and place them in the freezer for 10 minutes.

5 Meanwhile, heat a deep fat fryer filled with 3 inches of oil to 190°C/375°F.

6 Fry the mozzarella sticks for 1 minute each, until golden.

7 Drain, and serve with tomato sauce for dipping.

Chef's Note

Many people do not realise that you can make mozzarella from the milk of a Hippogriff, in the same way you can that of a buffalo. In fact, Hippogriff milk was used first, but the Italian wizard who invented the cheese was forced to attribute it to the local buffalo, to avoid arousing suspicion from Muggles.

Hot Chocolate Frog with Marshmallows

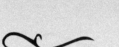

SERVES 4

Ingredients

- 600ml/1 pint milk
- 100g/3½oz Chocolate Frog, or plain chocolate, chopped
- 150ml/5floz double cream
- Handful Every Flavour Marshmallows

Method

1 Place the milk, chocolate and cream in a cauldron.

2 Heat gently, stirring continuously, until all the chocolate has melted, and the mixture is smooth.

3 Divide into 4 goblets, and serve with Every Flavour Marshmallows sprinkled liberally on top (try to pick the good ones!)

Chef's Note

Every Flavour Marshmallows are the new launch from Bertie Bott, following the overwhelming success of his Every Flavour Beans. Whilst they do add some excitement to the drink, you might find it more enjoyable to use Muggle marshmallows. After all, who wants earwax flavoured hot chocolate?

Fawkes' Fiery Vegetable Crisps

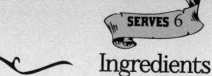

SERVES 6

Ingredients

- 2 parsnips
- 2 beetroots
- 1 carrot
- ½ butternut squash

- 1 tbsp olive oil
- ½ tsp salt
- 2 tsp chilli powder

Method

1 Pre-heat the oven to 180°C/350°F/Gas Mark 4.

2 Peel and thinly slice all the vegetables using a mandoline slicer.

3 Place the slices in a large bowl, and toss thoroughly with the oil and salt, to coat.

4 Line 1 or 2 large baking trays with parchment paper, and spread the vegetable slices over them in a single layer.

5 Roast the vegetable crisps in the oven for 8-10 minutes, turning halfway through.

6 Remove from the oven, and allow to cool. Sprinkle with chilli powder, and serve with your choice of dip (Fawkes prefers sour cream).

Chef's Note

These spicy vegetable crisps are Fawkes's favourite snack - he was even tucking into them the night he went to Harry's aid in the Chamber of Secrets. The thought of his unfinished plate of vegetable crisps waiting for him was great motivation to help Harry defeat the Basilisk quickly.

COMING SOON.....

the Unofficial

Harry Potter
Quiz Book